The
Canadian Style

A Guide to Writing and Editing

Department of the Secretary of State

The
Canadian Style

A Guide to Writing and Editing

Published by **Dundurn Press Limited** in co-operation with the Department of the Secretary of State and the Canadian Government Publishing Centre, Supply and Services Canada

Toronto and London
1985

Design and Production: Ron & Ron Design Photography
Typesetting: Linotext Inc.
Printing and Binding: T.H. Best Co.

Published by
Dundurn Press Limited
1558 Queen Street East
Toronto, Canada
M4L 1E8

Canadian Cataloguing in Publication Data

Main entry under title:
The Canadian style: a guide to writing and editing

Includes index.
ISBN 0-919670-93-8

1. Authorship—Handbooks, manual, etc.
2. Editing.   3. English language—Canada.
I. Canada. Secretary of State.

PN147.C36 1985   808'.02   C85-099335-0

Table of Contents

Chapter Two

Hyphenation: Compounding of words and word division 38

Chapter Three

Spelling 52

Chapter Four

Chapter Five

The Exclamation Mark

The Comma

The Semicolon

The Colon

Parentheses

Chapter Eight

Chapter Nine

Footnotes and Endnotes

Chapter Ten

Letters and memorandums 186

Letters

Memorandums

Chapter Eleven
Reports and minutes

Reports

Minutes

Chapter Twelve

Appendix I

Appendix II

Appendix III

Preface

The Department of the Secretary of State's Translation Bureau is pleased to present *The Canadian Style: A Guide to Writing and Editing* as the English-language counterpart of the *Guide du rédacteur de l'administration fédérale*, a French-language style manual published in 1983.

The production of this important work, undertaken by the Bureau some years ago, is a major contribution to the Department's role of supporting and fostering the use and development of Canada's official languages both within the federal public service and in other sectors of Canadian society. The Translation Bureau is the main agent for carrying out this part of the Department's mandate and devotes a considerable amount of its resources to standardization in language matters.

Public servants will find in *The Canadian Style* standards, recommendations and information that will enable them to ensure greater formal quality, consistency and clarity in government writing.

At the same time this work, representing as it does a successful attempt to capture many aspects of editorial style, should serve as an invaluable tool to all Canadians looking for a set of standards and a guide to solving the everyday problems of writing.

Benoît Bouchard

Secretary of State of Canada

Foreword

The Canadian Style: A Guide to Writing and Editing has been prepared to assist public servants at all levels whose work involves writing, editing or proofreading English-language material, as well as members of the general public who are called upon to prepare memorandums, reports or other documents in the course of their duties. It is designed to fill the need for a comprehensive, up-to-date Canadian manual that provides guidance in matters of usage and style.

This manual replaces the *Government of Canada Style Manual for Writers and Editors*, last reprinted in 1966. The new manual concentrates more heavily than did its predecessor on the specifically editorial aspects of writing, including abbreviations, hyphenation and compounding, spelling, capitalization, italics, numerical expressions, punctuation and quotations. Furthermore, the chapter on reference matter has been enlarged, sections on the preparation of letters, memorandums, reports and minutes have been included, and appendixes on geographical names and the elimination of sexual, racial and ethnic stereotyping in written communications have been added since these issues have been of increasing concern in recent years. However, unlike its predecessor, it does not treat graphs, tables and illustrations, which are properly the domain of the typographer.

On such questions as the use of periods with abbreviations, hyphenation and compounding, spelling and the capitalization of titles, Canadian practice varies considerably. Following examination of international standards, federal government documents and other Canadian material, we have sought to establish standards and thereby dispel the uncertainty surrounding these matters. In particular, we have selected the *Gage Canadian Dictionary* (1983) as the preferred reference work for spelling, hyphenation and compounding, and capitalization. But the standards and recommendations presented here should not be interpreted as categorical rejections of alternative forms which certain publishers may require. In this regard it should be borne in mind that the English language has long resisted attempts to impose on it a single, universal norm of style and usage.

A task as complex as that of producing *The Canadian Style* naturally demanded a great deal of time, patience and dedication from several members of the Translation Bureau. Peter Christensen and Hyman Bloom deserve special thanks for contributing first drafts of four chapters. The Bureau's Documentation Directorate made an invaluable contribution by reviewing the chapter on reference matter and making helpful suggestions and additions. We would also like to thank all those who took the time to comment on the first draft of this manual.

We hope that, in time, *The Canadian Style* will help to promote greater formal quality, consistency and clarity in written communications both within the federal government and outside.

Malcolm Williams	Frank Bayerl
Terminology and	Translation Operations
Documentation Branch	Branch
Translation Bureau	Translation Bureau
Project Co-ordinator	*Editor-in-Chief*
Writer-Editor	

Over To You . . .

With this publication we have attempted to meet the dual objective, established at the outset, of providing information and standardizing usage. But, like all such undertakings, our work may have fallen short of its objective. This edition will therefore be revised—a task in which we need your help. We would appreciate it if you would send your opinions and suggestions to the following address:

The Canadian Style
Linguistic Services Directorate
Translation Bureau
Secretary of State Department
Ottawa, Ontario
K1A 0M5

If, in order to back up a statement or justify a preference, you mention a reference that is not included in this guide, please send us a photocopy of it, if possible, along with the title and date of the publication from which you are quoting.

Thank you for your assistance!

One

Abbreviations

1

Abbreviations

1.01 Introduction

Abbreviations are a means of shortening recurrent terms and thereby ensuring a more concise, less repetitive style. The broad category of abbreviations may be subdivided into three types: abbreviations in the strict sense of the word, including the short forms of common nouns, Latin expressions, persons' names, months and days; acronyms and initialisms; and symbols such as those for metric units, which are uniform in many languages. All of these are discussed in the sections that follow.

Many commonly used words that are actually abbreviations are now rarely regarded as such. These include *ad, fridge, phone, exam, photo, cello, gym* and *pub*. Most words of this kind should be avoided in formal writing, although *cello* and *pub* are clearly exceptions to this rule.

In general, abbreviate words only when the short form will be immediately recognized by the reader, and ensure that the same abbreviation is used elsewhere in your text to represent the word or words involved. Some standard abbreviations such as *i.e., AD, IQ, ESP, CBC* and *MP* do not have to be spelled out because they are well known and in many cases occur as dictionary entries. However, unless you are confident that the reader will know exactly what the abbreviation stands for, write the term in full at first mention, with the abbreviation following in parentheses:

> **The forecast was made by an economist with the Economic Council of Canada** (ECC).

Thereafter the abbreviation may be used alone.

1.02 Periods

In recent years there has been a trend toward the omission of periods in abbreviations. This is particularly true of scientific and technical writing, but in many circles the practice has been adopted for general writing as well.

Do not use periods with the following:

- chemical symbols and mathematical abbreviations: H_2O, $NaCl$, *cos, log, tan;*
- metric unit and SI symbols (see 1.22);
- abbreviations for points of the compass, except with street addresses *(winds NNW* but *King St. E.);*
- other abbreviations consisting exclusively of upper-case letters or ending in an upper-case letter (except those for place names, personal names and legal references). These include acronyms and initialisms of all kinds: *YMCA, UN, MiG, PhD;*

• the military rank abbreviations used in the Department of National Defence (see 1.06).

1.03   Plurals

The plural of most abbreviations is formed by adding an *s* but not an apostrophe:

ADMs	ICPs
CAs	MPs
CRs	YMCAs

In cases where the resulting form would be ambiguous, it is better to add an apostrophe before the *s*:

c.o.d.'s	SIN's

The plural of certain reference abbreviations is formed differently:

l. (line)	ll. (lines)
p. (page)	p., pp. (pages)
f. (and the one following)	ff. (and those following)
c., ch. (chapter)	c., ch. (chapters)
MS (manuscript)	MSS (manuscripts)

but

s. (section)	ss. (sections)

Note that metric symbols do not change when used in the plural:

50 m	50 kg
18 L	20 kPa

1.04   Capital letters and hyphens

In general, an abbreviation is capitalized or hyphenated if the unabbreviated word or words are:

Lt.-Gov.	Lieutenant-Governor
MLA	Member of the Legislative Assembly
UBC	University of British Columbia

When an abbreviation is formed from letters most or all of which are part of a single word, it is capitalized, even though the full term is not:

ACTH	adrenocorticotrophic hormone
DNA	deoxyribonucleic acid
ESP	extrasensory perception
TB	tuberculosis
TV	television

See 1.16 for rules governing the capitalization of acronyms and initialisms.

1.05 Titles used with personal names

Use the following abbreviations for non-military titles preceding or following personal names:

Mr.	Dr.
Mrs.	Hon. (Honourable)
Ms.	Rt. Hon. (Right Honourable)
Messrs.	Msgr. (Monsignor)
Esq.	St. (Saint)
Jr.	Prof. (Professor)
Sr.	Rev. (Reverend)

Do not use *Mr., Mrs., Ms., Dr.* or *Esq.* with any other abbreviated title or with an abbreviation denoting an academic degree or honour:

Dr. Ruth Jones **or** Ruth Jones, MD
not
Mrs. **or** Dr. Ruth Jones, MD

Mr. Robert Smith **or** Robert Smith, Esq.
not
Mr. Robert Smith, Esq.

John Jones Jr.
not
Mr. John Jones Jr.

Abbreviate professional and official titles only when they are followed by the person's initials or first name as well as his or her surname:

Gen. J. A. Dextraze **but** General Dextraze
Dr. Ruth Jones **but** Doctor Jones
Prof. W. R. I. Shipley **but** Professor Shipley

Note that there are spaces between each period and the following initial or name. Avoid abbreviations such as *Chas.* for *Charles* and *Jos.* for *Joseph* which comprise more than just an initial letter. When reproducing a signature, however, retain the form used by the signatory.

Even when used to address someone in correspondence, *Rt. Hon., Hon.* and *Rev.* must be preceded by *the:*

The Rt. Hon. Brian Mulroney, Prime Minister of Canada
The Hon. Andrée Champagne, Minister of State for Youth
The Rev. John Smith

1.06   Military abbreviations

In the following table, the middle column gives the abbreviations used by the Department of National Defence and the right-hand column those recommended for use in non-military writing:[1]

Mobile and Air Commands

Officers

General	Gen	Gen.
Lieutenant-General	LGen	Lt.-Gen.
Major-General	MGen	Maj.-Gen.
Brigadier-General	BGen	Brig.-Gen.
Colonel	Col	Col.
Lieutenant-Colonel	LCol	Lt.-Col.
Major	Maj	Maj.
Captain	Capt	Capt.
Lieutenant	Lt	Lieut.
Second Lieutenant	2Lt	2nd Lieut.
Officer Cadet	OCdt	(not abbreviated)

Other ranks

Chief Warrant Officer	CWO	(not abbreviated)
Master Warrant Officer	MWO	(not abbreviated)
Warrant Officer	WO	(not abbreviated)
Sergeant	Sgt	(not abbreviated)
Master Corporal	MCpl	(not abbreviated)
Corporal	Cpl	Cpl.
Private	Pte	Pte.

Maritime Command

Admiral	Adm	(not abbreviated)
Vice-Admiral	VAdm	(not abbreviated)
Rear-Admiral	RAdm	(not abbreviated)
Commodore	Cmdre	(not abbreviated)
Captain	Capt	Capt.
Commander	Cdr	Cmdr.
Lieutenant-Commander	LCdr	Lt.-Cmdr.
Lieutenant	Lt	Lieut.
Sub-Lieutenant	SLt	Sub-Lieut.

---

1. See The Canadian Press, *Stylebook: A Guide for Writers and Editors*,
p. 9–11, for a comprehensive list of military abbreviations for general use.

1.07 University degrees, military decorations, honours, awards and memberships

These and other appropriate distinctions are given in abbreviated form after the name of the bearer:

Ingrid Butler, PhD, FRSC

The Hon. John Smith, BA, LLD

The Rev. Edwin O'Malley, SJ

Unless all honours have to be indicated for information or protocol purposes, no more than two abbreviations need follow a person's name—as, for example, in correspondence. In such cases select the two highest honours of different types and list them in the following order of precedence: first, distinctions conferred directly by the Crown (*VC, QC,* etc.); second, university degrees; and third, letters denoting membership in societies and other distinctions.

For further information and a comprehensive listing of such abbreviations, see the latest available editions of the *Canadian Almanac and Directory* and H. Measures, *Styles of Address*.

1.08 Geographical names

The names of provinces, territories and districts may be abbreviated when they follow the name of a city, town, village or geographical feature:

Toronto, Ont.   Mount Robson, B.C.

It is not necessary to use the provincial abbreviation after the names of well-known cities such as Vancouver, Winnipeg, Toronto and Fredericton. However, since the same name is often shared by several places in Canada and other parts of the English-speaking world (e.g. *Perth, Windsor*), add the appropriate abbreviation in cases where doubt could arise.

The following abbreviations are used officially for the names of provinces and territories in Canada. The right-hand column lists the abbreviations for use with postal code addresses. For general purposes, the traditional provincial abbreviations should continue to be used:

Alberta	Alta.	AB
British Columbia	B.C.	BC
Manitoba	Man.	MB
New Brunswick	N.B.	NB
Newfoundland	Nfld.	NF
Northwest Territories	N.W.T.	NT
Nova Scotia	N.S.	NS
Ontario	Ont.	ON
Prince Edward Island	P.E.I.	PE
Quebec	Que.	PQ
Saskatchewan	Sask.	SK
Yukon Territory	Y.T.	YT
(Labrador	Lab.	LB)

Do not abbreviate words such as *County, Fort, Mount, North, Point, Island, Port* and *Saint* used as part of a proper name, unless the official name for the location shows the abbreviated form:

Port Radium	St. John's, Nfld.
Fort Garry	Saint John, N.B.
Sable Island	

For further information on the official form of geographical names, see Appendix I, "Geographical Names."

1.09 Points of the compass

Abbreviate compass directions as follows:

N	NE
S	SW
E	NNW
W	ESE

The abbreviations *NE, NW, SE* and *SW* may be used to denote town and city divisions in general writing, but the words *north, south, east* and *west* should always be spelled out:

NW Toronto
Ottawa south

Note that a period follows these abbreviations in street addresses:

75 Booth St. N.

1.10 Latitude and longitude

The words *latitude* and *longitude* are never abbreviated when used alone or in ordinary prose:

What is the latitude of the Tropic of Cancer?
The wreck was found at 36°7′25″ north latitude and 15°24′00″ west longitude.

In technical work and when lists of co-ordinates are given, use the abbreviations *lat.* and *long.*:

lat. 42°15′30″ N	long. 89°17′45″ W
lat. 18°40′16″ S	long. 20°19′22″ E

1.11 Streets and buildings

Words such as *Street, Avenue, Place, Road, Square, Boulevard, Terrace, Drive, Court* and *Building* are spelled out in general writing but may be abbreviated in footnotes, endnotes, sidenotes, tables and addresses. If the word forms part of a longer name, do not abbreviate it under any circumstances:

He worked at the Journal Building.
Get off at Queen Street Station.

1.12 Parts of a book or document

Where there is a reference within the body of the text to a large subdivision of a publication or other document (e.g. *Appendix, Book, Chapter, Number, Part, Volume*) or to a smaller section that is part of a title *(Figure, Table, Plate)*, the word is capitalized and not abbreviated. Such a word is always followed by a number or letter, e.g. *Part 4, Table 14, Appendix C.*

Smaller subdivisions *(paragraph, line, page)* in the text are also written in full but are not capitalized except in main headings. See 4.33 for further treatment of these points. ·

In references—footnotes, endnotes, bibliographies and indexes—words referring to parts of a publication should, in the interest of conciseness, be abbreviated.

1.13 Latin terms

Beware of confusing and misusing the following abbreviations:

e.g.	for example	i.e.	that is, specifically, namely
etc.	and so on	et al.	and others (used in bibliographical references)

Note that the following Latin terms are not abbreviations and are never followed by a period unless they are placed at the end of a sentence:

ad	ex	in	per	sic
et	finis	par	pro	via

1.14 Scientific and technical terms

No attempt can be made in a manual of this kind to deal comprehensively with the vast array of technical and scientific abbreviations such as those for mathematical ratios and operations, physical quantities and constants or statistical formulas and notations. Most unabridged dictionaries list such abbreviations, and those working in specific disciplines should consult the appropriate manuals in their field.

In biology the Latin name for a genus is not abbreviated if used alone. When used with the species name, it is abbreviated as of the second reference. The species name is not abbreviated:

Clematis (genus)

Clematis virginiana (full scientific name at first reference)

C. virginiana (second and subsequent references)

1.15 Corporate names

Avoid using *Assoc., Bros., Co.* and *Corp.* within the body of your text. *Inc.* and *Ltd.*, however, may be used unless it is necessary to preserve the firm's full legal title.

All of the above forms may be freely used in footnotes, tables or bibliographical references.

1.16 Acronyms and initialisms

An acronym is a pronounceable word formed from the first letter or letters of a series of other words, such as *NATO, CUSO* or *NORAD*. An initialism is formed from the initial letters only of a series of words and may not be pronounceable as a word. Examples are *YMCA, OECD, IDRC* and *EEC*. The distinction is a fine one and is often overlooked in practice. Do not use periods or spacing between the letters of an acronym or initialism.

In general, acronyms are not preceded by the definite article:

The members of NATO rejected the idea.

CIDA provides grants, loans and lines of credit.

Usage varies with respect to initialisms. Those representing the names of organizations generally take the article, while those representing a substance, method or condition do not:

The CLRB is reviewing the case.

The unit has been using CPM for some time.

Use upper-case letters for acronyms or initialisms in their entirety, even if some of the component words or their parts are not normally capitalized, unless the organization concerned prefers lower case:

COMECON   Council for Mutual Economic Assistance

FORTRAN   formula translation

NORAD   North American Aerospace Defence
(Command)

Acronyms (but not initialisms) formed from company names are an exception:

Inco   International Nickel Company

Stelco   Steel Company of Canada Ltd.

Alcoa   Aluminum Company of America

but

RCA, IBM, CNCP Telecommunications, etc. (initialisms)

Common-noun acronyms treated as full-fledged words, such as *radar, laser* and *snafu,* are written entirely in lower case.

Note:
For a comprehensive list of the official acronyms and initialisms for federal government organizations, consult the Canadian government Treasury Board's *Administrative Policy Manual,* Chapter 470, Appendix C, "Titles of Organizations," June 1984.

1.17 Number and percentage symbols

Where the word *number* or *numbers* has to be represented within the body of the text, use *No.* or *Nos.* but not the symbol #:

> Nos. 56–86 are missing.

Use the percent sign (%) in economic, financial, statistical or other documents where figures are abundant. In material of a general nature containing isolated references to percentages, use the term *percent*.

1.18 Ampersand

The ampersand (&) is properly used only when it forms part of a corporate name:

> The publisher was Ginn & Co.
> The case is being defended by Collins, Smith, White & Jones.

Do not use the ampersand in federal department legal or applied titles:

> The Department of Indian and Northern Affairs
> Consumer and Corporate Affairs Canada

> **not**

> The Department of Indian & Northern Affairs
> Consumer & Corporate Affairs Canada

1.19 Social insurance number

The term *social insurance number* should be abbreviated SIN and be followed by the nine-digit number, with spacing but no hyphens between the sets of figures:

> SIN 123 456 789

It is incorrect to write *SIN number;* either write the term in full or use only the abbreviation. The same applies to ISBN *(International Standard Book Number)* and ISSN *(International Standard Serial Number)*.

1.20 Monetary units

When it is necessary to distinguish dollar amounts in one currency from those in another, use the appropriate symbol with the figure in question:

> Repayment of the loan will be in eighty instalments of
> C$650 each.

> Please enclose a cheque in the amount of US$100.

See 5.11 and 5.26 for further information on monetary units.

1.21 Months and days

Always spell out the names of the months in the body of your text and in footnotes, except when used in citations and references. They may be abbreviated in tabular matter and sidenotes. *May,* however, should not be abbreviated and *June* and *July* are shortened only in military writing.

The names of the days of the week are not abbreviated, except in tables.

1.22 The metric system and the International System of Units (SI)

The metric system is a decimal-based system of weights and measures, while the International System of Units (SI) is a broader system that includes units for physical quantities. Strictly speaking, metric and SI units are not abbreviated; they are represented by symbols that are identical in English, French and many other languages.

There are seven base units in SI:

Table 1

Quantity	Unit name	Symbol
length	metre	m
mass	kilogram	kg
time	second	s
electric current	ampere	A
thermodynamic temperature	kelvin	K
amount of substance	mole	mol
luminous intensity	candela	cd

In addition, a number of derived units are used. Like the kelvin and the ampere, almost all of them are named after scientists associated with a scientific discovery. When the symbol is used, its initial letter is capitalized; when written in full, the unit name is in lower case, e.g. *H* for *henry* and *F* for *farad*.
Exception:
Celsius takes an initial capital whether abbreviated or written in full.

The table below gives a complete list of derived units:

Table 2

Quantity	Unit name	Symbol
frequency	hertz	Hz
force	newton	N
pressure, stress	pascal	Pa
energy, work, quantity of heat	joule	J
power, radiant flux	watt	W
quantity of electricity, electric charge	coulomb	C

electric potential,		
potential difference,		
electromotive force	volt	V
electric capacitance	farad	F
electric resistance	ohm	O
electric conductance	siemens	S
magnetic flux	weber	Wb
magnetic flux density	tesla	T
inductance	henry	H
Celsius temperature	degree Celsius	°C
luminous flux	lumen	lm
illuminance	lux	lx
activity of radionuclides	becquerel	Bq
absorbed dose of		
ionizing radiation	gray	Gy

Multiples and sub-multiples of base units and derived units are expressed by adding one of the prefixes from the following table directly to the unit name:

Table 3

Prefix	Symbol	Means "multiply by"	Power
exa	E	1 000 000 000 000 000 000	10^{18}
peta	P	1 000 000 000 000 000	10^{15}
tera	T	1 000 000 000 000	10^{12}
giga	G	1 000 000 000	10^{9}
mega	M	1 000 000	10^{6}
kilo	k	1 000	10^{3}
hecto	h	100	10^{2}
deca	da	10	10^{1}
deci	d	0.1	10^{-1}
centi	c	0.01	10^{-2}
milli	m	0.001	10^{-3}
micro	μ	0.000 001	10^{-6}
nano	n	0.000 000 001	10^{-9}
pico	p	0.000 000 000 001	10^{-12}
femto	f	0.000 000 000 000 001	10^{-15}
atto	a	0.000 000 000 000 000 001	10^{-18}

The prefix and unit names are always spelled as one word:

centimetre	decagram
hectolitre	kilopascal

When symbols are used, the prefix and unit symbols are run together:

5 cm	4 dag
7 hL	13 kPa

When symbols consist entirely of letters, leave a full space between the quantity and the symbol:

45 kg not 45kg

When the symbol includes a non-letter character as well as a letter, leave no space:

32°C not 32° C or 32 °C

For the sake of clarity a hyphen may be inserted between a numeral and a symbol (see also 2.10):

35-mm film   a 60-W bulb

Unit symbols and prefixes are printed in roman type. They should always be in lower case, even when the rest of the text is in upper case:

SIBERIA DRIFTS 5 cm CLOSER TO ALASKA

Exceptions:
The symbol *L* for *litre* (to distinguish it from the numeral *1*) and, as mentioned above, those symbols derived from the names of scientists.

SI usage requires either that both figure and unit names be written in full or that both be abbreviated:

two metres or 2 m

not

2 metres or two m

When no specific figure is stated, write the unit name in full:

The means of transportation chosen depends on how many kilometres an employee has to travel to work.

Area and volume in the metric system are expressed by means of superscript numerals:

5 cm^2 20 m^3

Do not use unapproved metric abbreviations such as *cc* or *cu. cm* for *cubic centimetre (cm^3)*, *kilo* for *kilogram (kg)*, or *amp* for *ampere (A)*.

Because of their practical importance, the following additional units are approved for use with SI, although they do not strictly speaking form part of it:

Table 4

Quantity	Unit name	Symbol
time	minute	min
	hour	h
	day	d
	year	a
plane angle	degree	°
	minute	'
	second	"
	revolution	r
area	hectare	ha
volume	litre	L
mass	metric ton, tonne	t
linear density	tex	tex

Note that there is no standard symbol for *week* or *month*. These units should therefore always be spelled out in technical writing.

When a unit symbol is combined with a symbol for time, an oblique (/) separates the two:

80 km/h **not** 80 kmh **or** 80 kph

1800 r/min **not** 1800 rpm

The symbol μ (the Greek letter *mu*) should be drawn by hand if necessary, rather than typed as a *u*, as is sometimes done.

More detailed information on the metric system or SI can be found in CSA Special Publication Z372-1980, *Metric Editorial Handbook*, or the *Canadian Metric Practice Guide,* CAN3-Z234.1-79.

1.23   A note on the imperial system

Unit abbreviations in the imperial system take periods. Do not add an *s* to imperial weights and measures to form the plural. Area and volume in this system are usually expressed by means of the abbreviations *sq.* and *cu.* rather than a superscript numeral. A space should be left between *sq.* or *cu.* and the abbreviation that follows it:

8 in.   100 sq. ft.

11.6 sq. in.   20 cu. yd.

Two

Hyphenation

Compounding of words and word division

2

Hyphenation: compounding of words and word division

2.01 Introduction

A compound term is a combination of two or more words that, to varying degrees, have become unified in form and meaning through frequent use together. In many cases only one syllable in the compound is stressed. The trend over the years has been for the English compound to begin as two separate words, then be hyphenated and finally, if there is no structural impediment to union, become a single word written without a space or hyphen. Whatever its form, the compound frequently serves to avoid circumlocution and create a more concise style.

The existence of three different forms for compounds leads to considerable instability and variation in their presentation, and hyphenation has become one of the most controversial points of editorial style. Dictionaries vary widely in the forms they choose for specific compounds: "sheepdog" in the *Gage Canadian Dictionary*, "sheep dog" in *Webster's Third New International Dictionary* and "sheep-dog" in *The Concise Oxford Dictionary*, for example.

The modern tendency is to use hyphens sparingly, in situations where they are required to ensure clarity of meaning or of syntactical relationship. While Fowler states that "the hyphen is not an ornament but an aid to being understood, and should be employed only when it is needed for that purpose,"[1] Copperud notes that "it is worse to leave out the hyphen when it is desirable than to use it where it is not essential."[2] All authorities agree that the matter of hyphenation is one where the exercise of individual judgment is required, and the rules that follow are not intended to preclude its use. Where various authorities disagree, it has been thought desirable to err on the side of caution and recommend use of the hyphen for the sake of clarity.

In all that follows, another important distinction must be borne in mind: that between a compound term used before a noun **(attributively)** and one in some other position **(predicatively)**. As a general rule, terms that take a hyphen when preceding a noun do not take one in other positions, but there are enough exceptions to warrant their being noted, and this is done below.

---

1. H. W. Fowler, *A Dictionary of Modern English Usage*, p. 255.
2. Roy H. Copperud, *American Usage and Style: The Consensus*, p. 188.

Although they do not form true compounds, prefixes and suffixes are treated in this chapter because they pose similar problems with respect to hyphenation.

Consult the *Gage Canadian Dictionary* for the form of frequently used compounds (including those based on prefixes and suffixes), and then follow the rules below for those not found in *Gage*.

2.02 Compound nouns and nouns in compounds

a) Hyphenate two nouns representing different but equally important functions, i.e. where the hyphen denotes the relationship "both A and B":

soldier-statesman	comedy-ballet
city-state	dinner-dance

b) Hyphenate nouns normally written as two words, when they have a modifier and when ambiguity would otherwise result:

colour filter **but** red colour-filter

letter writers **but** public letter-writers

Similarly, compound nouns normally written as a single word must be separated into their component parts and then joined to their modifier by a hyphen when the modifier applies only to the first component:

ironworker **but** structural-iron worker

housekeeper **but** lodging-house keeper

c) Hyphenate compound units of measurement made by combining single units which stand in a mathematical relationship to each other:

car-miles	light-year
kilowatt-hours	person-year

d) Hyphenate compounds that include a finite verb:

a has-been	a stay-at-home
a sing-along	a stick-in-the-mud

e) Hyphenate nouns of family relationship formed with *great* and *in-law:*

mother-in-law	great-grandfather

but

foster father	half brother

2.03 Nouns with adjectives and participles

a) Hyphenate noun-plus-adjective compounds, whether used attributively or predicatively:

duty-free goods	The goods were duty-free.
tax-exempt bonds	The bonds are tax-exempt.

b) Hyphenate noun-plus-participle compounds in all positions:

snow-capped mountains   The mountains are snow-capped.
a time-consuming activity   This activity is time-consuming.

Exceptions:
There are a number of them, including *handmade* and *handwritten*.

c) Do not hyphenate compound nouns consisting of a noun plus a gerund (present participle used as a noun); they may be written as one or as separate words:

decision making	housekeeping
power sharing	shipbuilding
problem solving	sightseeing

See 2.04(e) for such compounds used adjectivally.

2.04 Compound adjectives; adjectives and participles in compounds

a) Hyphenate adjective-plus-noun and participle-plus-noun compounds modifying another noun, when ambiguity might otherwise result:

cold-storage vaults	large-scale development
full-time jobs	sustained-yield management

When the compound is used predicatively, retain the hyphen only when the expression remains adjectival:

The development was large-scale.
His position is full-time.

but

Development proceeded on a large scale.
He works full time.

b) Hyphenate compound adjectives made up of two adjectives that describe a colour without the suffix *ish*, whether they are placed before or after the noun (compounds which include the suffix are hyphenated only when they precede the noun):

It was covered with blue-green algae.
It was blue-green.
The leaves were bluish green.
The tree had bluish-green leaves.

Do not hyphenate adjectives indicating a specific shade (even if they precede the noun):

dark green paint
a bright red dress

c) Hyphenate adjective-plus-participle compounds, whether used before the noun or after it:

> an odd-sounding name
> The name was rather odd-sounding.
> a smooth-talking salesman
> The visitor was smooth-talking.

d) Hyphenate compounds made up of an adjective plus a noun plus the ending *ed* in any position in the sentence:

> able-bodied   many-sided
> freckle-faced   short-handed

e) Hyphenate two-word compound adjectives consisting of a noun plus a gerund when they precede the noun:

> the decision-making process   a profit-sharing plan
> a problem-solving approach   a tape-recording session

See also 2.03(c).

f) Hyphenate compound adjectives whose final constituent is an adverb of direction or place (*in, out, down, up,* etc.) when they precede the noun:

> an all-in price   a built-up area
> an all-out war   the trickle-down theory

g) Hyphenate compound adjectives made up of a preposition and a noun:

> on a per-gram basis   in-service courses
> out-of-province benefits an in-house organ

h) Hyphenate a compound adjective one of whose constituents is a finite verb:

> a would-be writer   a pay-as-you-go approach

i) Hyphenate phrases of more than two words, at least one of which is an adverb or preposition, used as attributive adjectives:

> the cost-of-living index
> a long-drawn-out affair
> a subject-by-subject analysis
> a work-to-rule campaign
> an up-to-date approach
> on-the-job training

j) Do not hyphenate French or foreign words in italics, proper nouns or words in quotation marks:

> a Portage Avenue address
> a Privy Council decision
> a New York State chartered bank
> a *dolce far niente* attitude
> *a priori* reasoning
> a "take it or leave it" attitude

k) Do not hyphenate chemical terms used as adjectives:

> a sodium chloride solution   a calcium nitrate deposit

l) Hyphenate compound proper adjectives that form a true compound, but do not hyphenate those in which a proper adjective is combined with a simple modifier:

> Anglo-Saxon period   Latin American governments
> Franco-Prussian War   Middle Eastern affairs
> Austro-Hungarian Empire   North American interests
> French-Canadian cuisine   Central European powers

2.05 Verbs

a) Compound verbs may be either hyphenated or written solid. The only safe rule is to check *Gage:*

> freeze-dry   mass-produce
> age-harden   spoon-feed

> **but**

> waterproof   downgrade
> sidetrack   proofread

b) If the infinitive form of the verb (e.g. to *air-condition*) is hyphenated, retain the hyphen in all other forms, except as illustrated in (c):

> The theatre was air-conditioned.
> You need an air-conditioning expert.
> Please double-space the letter.

c) Hyphenate gerunds (participles functioning as nouns) formed from hyphenated compound verbs only if they are followed by a noun object:

> Dry cleaning is the simplest way to clean a sweater.

> **but**

> Dry-cleaning the sweater should remove the stain.

Air conditioning is sometimes needed in summer.

but

Cost must be considered in deciding whether air-conditioning the building is feasible.

2.06 Adverbs in compounds

a) Adverb-plus-participle compounds are among the most troublesome. Those in which the adverb ends in *ly* are not hyphenated:

richly embroidered   fully employed

In other cases, hyphenate before the noun:

far-reaching events   ill-educated person
ever-changing tides   well-fed cattle

When the compound follows the noun or pronoun and contains a past participle, omit the hyphen:

She is well known.
This applicant is ill suited for the job.

When the compound follows the noun or pronoun and contains a present participle, omit the hyphen if the participle has a verbal function, but retain it if it is adjectival in nature:

The narrative is fast-moving. (adjectival)

but

The narrative is fast moving toward a climax. (verbal)

b) Do not hyphenate compounds consisting of an adverb or adverbial phrase plus an adjective unless there is a danger of misreading:

equally productive means
a reasonably tall tree
an all too complacent attitude

2.07 Prefixes

a) Hyphenate a prefix joined to a proper noun:

mid-July   sub-Arctic
neo-Christian   trans-Siberian
pro-Canadian   un-American

Exceptions:
transatlantic and *transpacific*.

b) Hyphenate expressions beginning with the prefixes *ex* (when it means "former"), *self*, *quasi* and *all*, where used to form adjectives or nouns, and those beginning with *quasi* used to form adjectives:

all-inclusive	quasi-judicial
all-powerful	quasi-stellar
ex-wife	self-assured
ex-premier Robichaud	self-control

but

quasi corporation

quasi humour

However, when *self* is the base word to which a suffix is added, do not hyphenate:

selfish	selfhood
selfsame	selfless

c) Most words beginning with the following prefixes are written as one word: *after, ante, anti, bi, co, counter, de, down, extra, infra, inter, intra, iso, macro, micro, multi, over, photo, poly, post, pre, pro, pseudo, re, retro, semi, stereo, sub, super, trans, tri, ultra, un, under* and *up*:

afterthought	isometric	retroactive
antecedent	macrocosm	semiquaver
antiballistic	microscope	stereophonic
bimonthly	multistage	subspecies
covalent	overestimate	supernatural
counterclockwise	photovoltaic	transcontinental
decertify	polyurethane	triennial
downturn	postnatal	ultrasound
extrasensory	preposition	unassuming
infrastructure	proconsul	underrate
interstellar	pseudonym	upswing
intramural	readapt	

However, there are many exceptions. Check the *Gage Canadian Dictionary* when in doubt, and see below and 2.07(a) for specific types of exception.

Use a hyphen when the word following the prefix begins with the same vowel as the one with which the prefix ends, or when the compound's appearance would be confusing without the hyphen:

anti-inflation	re-educate
co-operation	semi-invalid
co-author	de-icing

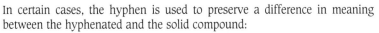

In certain cases, the hyphen is used to preserve a difference in meaning between the hyphenated and the solid compound:

re-cover (cover again)	re-solve (solve again)
recover (get better, get back)	resolve (settle)
re-create (create again)	re-sign (sign again)
recreate (take recreation)	resign (quit a job)

d) Write metric unit compounds as one word:

centimetre	kilokelvins
gigagram	milliampere

e) Hyphenate chemical terms preceded by an italicized prefix:

cis-dimethylethylene

β-lactose

2.08 *Any, every, no* and *some*

The words *any, every, no* and *some* form solid compounds when combined with *body, thing* and *where:*

anybody	everybody	nobody	somebody
anything	everything	nothing	something
anywhere	everywhere	nowhere	somewhere

However, when *one* is the second element, write *no* as a separate, unhyphenated word in all situations and write *any* and *every* as separate, unhyphenated words if *one* is followed by a prepositional phrase beginning with *of:*

No one came.

Any one of us can do it.

Each and every one of you must take the blame.

but

Someone told me.

Everyone is in agreement.

Anyone can participate.

2.09 Suffixes

a) like

Write these compounds as one word, except where this would result in a double *l* and where the compound is a temporary one coined for a specific purpose or text:

businesslike	ladylike
childlike	lifelike

but

nut-like	petal-like

b) wide

Since usage depends on the degree of familiarity of the compound, no general rule can be stated. Note the following:

worldwide   storewide

but

Canada-wide   province-wide
industry-wide   nation-wide

c) Hyphenate compounds made up of a numerical expression plus *odd* or *strong:*

sixty-odd   thirty-strong

d) Write compounds with *fold* and *score* as one word, except when the numerical expression itself already has a hyphen:

twofold   sixtyfold
threescore   fourscore

but

twenty-two-fold

2.10 Numerals and units of measurement

a) Hyphenate compound cardinal and ordinal numerals from *twenty-one (twenty-first)* to *ninety-nine (ninety-ninth)* when written out:

There are twenty-nine members on the committee.

b) Hyphenate a compound adjective in which one element is a cardinal or ordinal numeral and the other a noun or adjective:

a five-kilometre trek   a two-car family
a first-class coach   a third-rate play
a 60-W bulb

But do not hyphenate before a symbol that is not a letter, and do not hyphenate a modifier in which the numeral, written in full, is itself a compound:

a 100°C thermometer
a two hundred and fifty hectare farm

In such cases as the second example, the abbreviated form (e.g. *a 250-ha farm*) should be used if at all possible.

See 5.05 and 5.08 for further information.

c) Do not hyphenate a possessive noun preceded by a numerical expression:

one week's pay   40 hours' work
three weeks' vacation   10 months' leave

d) Hyphenate expressions of time of day as follows when numerals are written out:

eight-thirty   four-twenty

eight thirty-five   four twenty-six

2.11 Fractions

Hyphenate fractions used as modifiers and written in full, unless the numerator or denominator already contains a hyphen:

a one-third share

twenty-fiftieths calcium

but

one thirty-second

twenty-nine fiftieths calcium (In this case figures are preferable.)

Do not hyphenate fractions used as nouns:

Four fifths of the load was wheat, and one fifth barley.

2.12 The suspended compound

Hyphenate as follows when an element common to successive compound adjectives is omitted:

first- and second-class fares

high- and low-pressure turbine

interest- or revenue-producing schemes

short- and long-term plans

two-, four- and six-metre widths

2.13 Points of the compass

Compass directions consisting of two points are written as one word, but a hyphen is used after the first point in those consisting of three points:

northeast   north-northeast

southwest   south-southwest

2.14 Titles of office

Hyphenate compounds with the endings *elect* and *designate:*

president-elect   minister-designate

Hyphenate most titles beginning with the prefix *vice,* and the names of certain military and administrative positions in which a noun is followed by another noun, an adjective or a prepositional phrase:

vice-president   Commander-in-Chief

vice-chairman   Secretary-General

aide-de-camp   Lieutenant-Governor

There are, however, many common exceptions to this rule, e.g.:

Governor General	Solicitor General
Governor in Council	Auditor General
Judge Advocate General	Viceroy

Note that in Canadian usage the hyphen is used in compounds designating military ranks such as *Lieutenant-General, Vice-Admiral* and *Rear-Admiral,* while the American practice is to omit the hyphen. Similarly, the official title of the second-highest-ranking official of the United States is *Vice President.*

2.15 Figures and single letters

Hyphenate figures or single letters and the words they modify:

A-bomb	T-shirt
S-hook	U-turn
1,2-dimethylbutylene	2,4-D

But do not hyphenate a compound adjective when the second element is a letter or figure:

Class II railroad	Grade A milk

2.16 Plurals of compound terms

a) In forming the plurals of compound terms, the significant word is pluralized. If both words are of equal significance, both are pluralized. If no one word is significant in itself, the last one takes the plural form:

attorneys general	women writers
brigadier-generals	assistant chiefs of staff
trade unions	forget-me-nots
judge advocates	hand-me-downs
men drivers	courts-martial

b) When a noun is hyphenated with a preposition, the plural is formed on the noun:

fillers-in	hangers-on
goings-on	makers-up

c) When neither word of a compound is a noun, the plural is formed on the last word:

also-rans	go-betweens
run-ins	higher-ups

d) Add s to nouns ending in *ful:*

spoonfuls	cupfuls

2.17 Word division

In order to ensure clear, unambiguous presentation, avoid dividing words at the end of a line as much as possible. If word division is necessary, good sense and readability should be your guides. There are few absolute rules, but the accepted practice is summarized below.[3]

a) Usually, words may be divided between syllables (the *Gage Canadian Dictionary* shows syllabication clearly for all its entries), but not all syllable breaks are acceptable as end-of-line breaks, as rules (b) to (m) explain.

b) Two-letter syllables should not be carried over to the next line *(fully,* not *ful-ly; stricken,* not *strick-en).* Similarly, final syllables in which a liquid *l* is the only audible vowel sound should not be carried over *(pos-sible,* not *possi-ble; prin-ciples,* not *princi-ples).*

c) Words of one syllable or words in which the second "syllable" contains only a silent *e (aimed, helped, vexed,* etc.) should not be divided.

d) One-letter word divisions are not permissible. Such words as *again, item, enough* and *even* should not be divided.

e) Avoid awkward divisions, such as would result from attempting to divide *every, only, eighteen* and *people.*

f) Divide between a prefix and a following letter *(pre-fix, re-location).*

g) Divide a word between the root and the suffix *(care-less, convert-ible, world-wide).*

h) When a consonant is double, divide it for purposes of word division *(equip-ping, rub-ber).*

i) Avoid misleading breaks that may cause the reader to confuse one word with another, as in *read-just* and *reap-pear.* Similarly, such words as *women* and *often* should be left unbroken.

j) Hyphenated compounds should be broken only at the hyphen, if possible *(court-martial,* not *court-mar-tial).* A compound written as one word should be divided between its elements *(hot-house, sail-boat).*

k) Most words ending in *ing* may be divided at that syllable; when the final consonant is doubled before *ing,* however, the second consonant is carried over *(bid-ding, control-ling).* When the verb has an *l* preceded by a consonant, carry over the letter preceding the *l (han-dling, dwin-dling, tin-kling).*

l) Do not divide abbreviations, numbers and contractions *(UNDP, 235 006 114.37, won't).* Abbreviations used with figures should not be separated from the figures *(16 kg, 0°C, s.4, 11:55 a.m.).*

m) The last word on a page should never be divided.

---

3. See also P. Kirby, "English Word Division," *Termiglobe,* VII, 4 (November 1984): 24.

Three

Spelling

3

Spelling

3.01 Introduction

Spelling poses a major problem in English because it is so unphonetic and because the rules that can be formulated nearly always have significant exceptions. In addition, there are hundreds of words that have variant spellings in different parts of the English-speaking world, the principal cleavage being between the United Kingdom and the United States. Partly as a result of our historical links with Britain and our proximity to the United States, Canadian spelling has tended to waver between the forms used in these two countries, so that, to this day, there is no clearly established Canadian standard.[1]

While a list of words that have variant spellings in British and American practice would run into the hundreds and still not be exhaustive, the great majority of them fall into a few well-defined classes, as listed below. The British variants are given in the left-hand column, the American in the right-hand column:

- verbs ending in *ise/ize* and their derived forms:

civilise, civilisation	civilize, civilization
organise, organisation	organize, organization
specialise, specialisation	specialize, specialization

- nouns ending in *our/or:*

colour, honour, favour, etc.	color, honor, favor, etc.

- nouns ending in *re/er:*

centre, fibre, theatre, etc.	center, fiber, theater, etc.

- verbs with single *l*/double *l* and their derivatives:

instil	instill
fulfil, fulfilment	fulfill, fulfillment
enrol, enrolment	enroll, enrollment

- nouns in *ce/se:*[2]

defence, offence, pretence	defense, offense, pretense

---

1. M. Orkin, *Speaking Canadian English*, p. 150.

2. British spelling also makes a distinction between certain noun and verb forms that is not maintained in American spelling. Thus, British *licence* (noun), *license* (verb) and *practice* (noun), *practise* (verb); American *license* and *practice* for both forms.

• double *l*/single *l* in the past tense of verbs:

| counselled, labelled, travelled | counseled, labeled, traveled |

• treatment of the digraphs *ae* and *oe* in words from Latin and Greek:

| anaemia, encyclopaedia | anemia, encyclopedia |
| diarrhoea, oecumenical | diarrhea, ecumenical |

The spelling authority recommended by this manual is the *Gage Canadian Dictionary* (1983), since it reflects the usage of the majority of federal government departments and agencies more closely than do the *Webster's* or *Oxford* dictionaries, is based on research into Canadian usage, and contains specifically Canadian terms. When it lists two spellings for a word in the same entry, choose the one entered first—with the exception that where a choice exists[3] the form in *our,* found in the publications of most federal organizations and prescribed by order-in-council,[4] should be used. Sometimes the entries are listed separately; the primary spelling is the one followed by the definition, while the variant simply refers the reader to the primary spelling entry. For scientific and technical words not in *Gage,* check *Webster's Third New International Dictionary* (1981) or *Webster's Ninth New Collegiate Dictionary* (1983).

In light of these recommendations, the following variant spellings in the above list should be used: endings in *ize, ization, our, re,* single *l* (as in *instil*) and *ce;* single *l* in words such as *enrolment; ll* in *travelled,* etc.; and *e* for digraphs (exception: *aesthetic*).

The rules and lists of words given in this chapter are intended to supplement, not replace the use of the *Gage Canadian Dictionary*. The important point with respect to spelling is to be consistent in your written work unless some good reason exists for using variant or archaic spellings.

3.02   Frequently misspelled words

The following is a list of words that are often misspelled. The letters that are usually the object of the errors—through inversion, omission, doubling, addition or substitution—are in boldface:

ab**h**or	a**pp**e**ll**ant	cart**i**lage
ab**y**smal	ar**c**tic	cen**s**us
acco**mm**odate	arg**u**ment	Chil**e** (the country)
ac**q**uaintance	a**tt**orney	chlorophy**ll**
a**gg**ressive	a**w**kward	co**h**erent, co**h**erence
a**ll** right	ca**n**ister	commi**t**ment
an**o**malous	Cari**bb**ean	compara**t**ive

---

3. In some words, such as *horror, tremor, pallor* and *terror,* there is no choice. It should also be noted that not all derivatives of *our* words have the u. Some are regarded as being derived directly from Latin forms and are spelled accordingly: *coloration, honorary, honorific,* etc.

4. An order-in-council dated June 12, 1890 stated that "in all official documents, in the Canada Gazette, and in the Dominion Statutes, the English practice of *our* endings shall be followed."

concomitant
connection
consensus
consistent, consistency
corollary
correspondence
crystallographic
Dene (no accents in English)
descend
desiccate
develop
diarrhea
diphtheria
disappoint
discernible
domain **not** domaine
dysentery
ecstasy
embarrass
exaggerate
excerpt
exhilarate
existent, existence
exonerate
exorbitant **not** exhorbitant
Filipino
focus
foreseen
gauge
genealogy
grammar
guerrilla
harass
hereditary
hemorrhage

histogram
hypocrisy
hypothesis
independent, independence
inscribe
Inuk
Inuit
indispensable
infinitesimal
inoculate
insistent, insistence
iridescent
irrelevant
laboratory
liaison
lightning
liquefy
marshal
measure
medicine
memento
Métis
minuscule
Mississippi
misspell
moccasin
Morocco
naphtha
negotiation
nickel
occasional
occurrence
ophthalmology
paraffin
parallel

pastime
perinatal
permissible
Philippines
polyethylene
polystyrene
polyurethane
possession
precede
preferential
privilege
proceed
pronunciation
ptomaine
rarefy
recommendation
reminiscent
resistant, resistance
responsible
rheumatism
sacrilegious
separate
siege
soybean
spatial
stochastic
supersede
tariff
tendency
thorough
threshold
until
weird
withhold
written

3.03 Metric and SI units

The Canadian Standards Association has established preferred spellings or terms for a number of metric units and prefixes for which variants exist: *deca* (not *deka*), *gram* (not *gramme*), *litre* (not *liter*) and *tonne* or *metric ton* (not *metric tonne*).

In two cases the final vowel of a unit prefix is omitted: *megohm* and *kilohm*. In other cases where the unit name begins with a vowel, both vowels are retained.

Note that *meter* is the spelling for a measuring device, while *metre* is the unit of length.

Note also that the singular and plural of the following unit names are identical: *hertz, lux* and *siemens*.

3.04　Homonyms and similar-sounding words

Many words are misspelled because they are confused with similar-sounding and similarly spelled words which, in fact, have a different meaning. In the following list of word pairs (and one group of three), information is given in parentheses to indicate which spelling should be used in a particular context:

affect (influence)	effect (verb: bring about, result in; noun: consequence, impact)
allusion (reference)	illusion (misleading appearance)
all ready (prepared)	already (previously)
ascent (climb)	assent (agreement)
bloc (group of persons, companies or nations)	block (group of things; obstruct; solid piece, etc.)
born (of birth)	borne (carried)
breach (gap; violation)	breech (lower part)
broach (pointed tool or rod; begin to talk about)	brooch (type of jewellery)
canvas (cloth)	canvass (solicit)
capital (city; very significant)	capitol (government building in U.S.A.)
carat (unit of mass for precious stones)	caret (proofreader's mark) karat (unit used to specify proportion of gold in alloy)
cast (actors; verb meanings)	caste (exclusive social class)
censor (check the morality of; person who does this)	censure (criticize, blame; criticism)
chord (music; geometry; engineering)	cord (other uses)
complement (complete; that which completes)	compliment (praise)

councillor (member of a council)	counsellor (adviser; lawyer)
dependant (noun)	dependent (adjective)
discreet (prudent, tactful)	discrete (distinct, separate)
dyeing (colouring)	dying (approaching death)
elicit (draw forth)	illicit (unlawful)
envelop (verb)	envelope (noun)
faze (disturb)	phase (stage, period)
flair (talent)	flare (flame, light)
forbear (hold back)	forebear (ancestor)
foreword (preface)	forward (ahead)
hoard (save up)	horde (crowd)
immanent (inherent)	imminent (about to occur)
inequity (unfairness)	iniquity (sin)
its (belonging to it)	it's (it is)
loath (adjective)	loathe (verb)
loose (set free; untight, etc.)	lose (mislay; forfeit)
mantel (shelf above fireplace)	mantle (cloak, etc.)
mucous (adjective)	mucus (noun)
ordinance (law)	ordnance (military weapons)
pedal (operate levers with feet; activation device)	peddle (sell, hawk)
personal (individual, private)	personnel (staff)
phosphorous (adjective)	phosphorus (noun)
principal (chief, main, leading; school administrator)	principle (rule)
prophecy (noun)	prophesy (verb)
sceptic (one who doubts)	septic (purified, purifying)
stationary (fixed, motionless)	stationery (writing materials)
therefor (for this purpose or thing)	therefore (for that reason, consequently)
troop (soldiers)	troupe (actors, performers)
waive (give up, forego)	wave (move up and down, etc.)

3.05 Words with *ei* and *ie*

The jingle "*i* before *e* except after *c* or when sounded as *a* as in *neighbour* and *weigh*" covers the rule.

Exceptions:

either	heifer	neither
foreign	height	seize
forfeit	leisure	sovereign
weird		

3.06 Verbs ending in *sede, ceed* and *cede*

Supersede is the only verb ending in *sede. Exceed, proceed* and *succeed* are the only common verbs ending in *ceed*. Some verbs ending in *cede* are:

accede	concede	recede
antecede	intercede	secede
cede	precede	

3.07 *Able/ible* and *ative/itive* endings

There is no basic rule for these endings. However, if there is a corresponding word ending in *ation,* the ending is usually *able* or *ative;* if the corresponding word ends in *sion* or *tion* not preceded by *a*, the ending is usually *ible* or *itive:*

affirmation	affirmative
duration	durable
information	informative
competition	competitive
division	divisible
reproduction	reproducible

3.08 Final consonants doubled before a suffix

Double the final consonant before a suffix beginning with a vowel or *y* in a word of one syllable ending in a single consonant preceded by a single vowel:

bed	bedded	rot	rotted
dip	dipped	scrub	scrubbing
fit	fitted	sit	sitting
flit	flitting	stop	stopping
mad	madden	wet	wetting

Exceptions:
Do not double the final consonant in a word of one syllable if the vowel sound is long:

boat	boating
light	lighting
stoop	stooping
read	reading

The final consonant is usually doubled in words of more than one syllable ending in a single consonant preceded by a single vowel, if the accent is on the last syllable and the suffix begins with a vowel:

acquit	acquittal
commit	committal
occur	occurrence
rebel	rebellion
regret	regretted
transmit	transmitted

3.09 Words ending in *n*

When the suffix *ness* is added to a word ending in *n*, a double *n* is formed:

even	evenness	keen	keenness
green	greenness	sudden	suddenness

3.10 Combinations with *all*

The final *l* is usually dropped when *all* is used as a prefix:

all together	altogether
all ready	already

but

all right

3.11 Words ending in a silent *e*

The final *e* is usually dropped before a suffix beginning with a vowel:

debate	debatable	make	makable
desire	desirable	move	movable
dine	dining	rate	ratable
excite	excitable	sale	salable
like	likable	size	sizable
love	lovable	subdue	subduing

but

age	ageing
mile	mileage

However, when *e* follows *c* or *g* it is retained before the vowels *a* and *o* to preserve the soft sound of these consonants:

change	changeable **but** changing
courage	courageous
gauge	gaugeable **but** gauging
knowledge	knowledgeable
notice	noticeable **but** noticing
peace	peaceable
trace	traceable **but** tracing

Note that the *e* is retained even before *i* in some cases in order to distinguish a word from a similarly spelled one or to preserve a particular pronunciation:

dyeing	singeing
shoeing	toeing

Words ending in a silent *e* generally retain the *e* before a suffix beginning with a consonant:

complete	completeness
hope	hopeless
waste	wasteful
whole	wholesome

Exceptions:

duly	truly
subtly	wholly

abridgment   acknowledgment   judgment

3.12 Words ending in *c*

In words ending in a *c* having the sound of *k*, add *k* before *e*, *i* or *y*:

picnic	picnicking
panic	panicky
Quebec	Quebecker
traffic	trafficking

3.13 Verbs ending in *ie*

In verbs ending in *ie*, change *ie* to *y* before *ing*:

die	dying
lie	lying
tie	tying
vie	vying

3.14   Words ending in *y*

In words ending in *y* preceded by a consonant, change the *y* to *i* before a suffix, unless the suffix itself begins with *i*:

heavy	heaviest
lively	livelihood
salary	salaried
necessary	necessarily

but

copyist	flying
denying	trying

Note the distinction between *dryer* (something or someone that dries) and *drier* (comparative of *dry*).

Words ending in *y* preceded by a vowel generally retain the *y* before a suffix:

annoy	annoyance	annoying
pay	payable	paying

3.15   Words ending in *ise* and *ize*

The following are the only common words ending in ise:

advertise	compromise	exercise	premise
advise	demise	franchise	reprise
apprise	despise	guise	revise
arise	devise	improvise	supervise
chastise	disguise	incise	surmise
circumcise	enterprise	merchandise	surprise
comprise	excise	mortise	televise

To this list should be added all words with *wise* as a suffix.

3.16   Plural forms of nouns

Note the following singular and plural forms:

addendum	addenda
analysis	analyses
appendix	appendixes
basis	bases
bureau	bureaus
bus	buses
crisis	crises
criterion	criteria
erratum	errata

focus	focuses (*not* focusses, *which is the preferred verb form*)
formula	formulas
gas	gases (*not* gasses, *which is the verb form*)
hypothesis	hypotheses
index	indexes *(of a book)* **or** indices *(in mathematics, statistics)*
medium	mediums **or** media *(check dictionary for plural form to use in a given context)*
memorandum	memorandums
parenthesis	parentheses
phenomenon	phenomena
plateau	plateaus
surplus	surpluses

Many other English words form their plural irregularly, including some of those ending in *y, o, f* and *fe*.

Four

Capitalization

4

Capitalization

4.01 Introduction

Capital letters have three basic uses, of which nearly all others may be regarded as particular cases: (1) to give emphasis, as in official titles and initial words; (2) to distinguish proper nouns and adjectives from common ones; and (3) to highlight words in headings and captions. The material below concerns problems arising from uses (1) and (2). The third use is discussed in 11.12.

In English the first letter of certain words is capitalized to give emphasis and to clarify sentence structure and meaning for the reader. This chapter gives rules to define which words require capitals, but it should be kept in mind that editorial practice differs considerably on this subject, depending on the degree of formality of the writing, the intended audience and the house style of the publication.

In order to ensure consistency in your own style, follow the rules below, which are intended to be applicable to most types of writing, and consult the *Gage Canadian Dictionary*, which gives the upper-case use of many words.

4.02 Initial words

a) Capitalize the first word of a sentence or sentence equivalent:

> There are no other constraints.
> Come.
> What a pity!
> Why?
> Exit
> All rights reserved

b) The first word of a line of poetry is traditionally capitalized, but some modern poets do not follow this practice. It is therefore best to check the original and respect the poet's preference.

c) Capitalize the first word of a direct quotation that is itself a complete sentence:

> The candidates said, "We are in favour of a free vote on the death penalty."

Do not use a capital if the quotation is merely a sentence fragment or is worked into the structure of the sentence:

> The candidates said that they were "in favour of a free vote on the death penalty."

For more detailed information on quotations, see Chapter 8.

d) Capitalize the first word of a complete sentence enclosed in parentheses when it stands alone, but not when it is enclosed within another sentence:

> The speaker concluded by citing facts and figures to support her contention. (Details may be found on p. 37.)

> The increasing scarcity of the species is attributable to overfishing (statistics will be found in the appendix), to acid rain and to other factors outlined in the report.

e) Capitalize the first word of a direct question within a sentence:

> The question to be asked in every case is: Does the writer express himself or herself clearly?

f) Do not capitalize the first word after a colon unless it begins a direct question (see 4.02(e) above) or a formal statement, introduces a fairly distinct idea or is intended to have special emphasis:

> There are several possibilities: for example, the Director General might resign.

> The jury finds as follows: The defendant is guilty as charged on all counts.

> In conclusion, I answer the question asked at the outset: Revenue will be greater this year than in the past three years.

g) The word following a question mark or exclamation mark may or may not be capitalized, depending on how closely the material it introduces is considered to be related to what precedes:

> What a piece of work is man! how noble in reason! how infinite in faculty!

> Progress where? or, even more fundamentally, progress for whom?

> What factors contributed to the decline of Rome? Did the barbarian invasions play a significant part?

h) The personal pronoun *I* and the vocative *O* are always capitalized in English; *oh* is capitalized only when it begins a sentence or stands alone.

4.03 Personal names

Capitalize proper names and epithets that accompany or replace them:

John Diefenbaker	Peter the Great
Margaret Thatcher	the Sun King

When *O'* forms part of a proper name, it and the first letter after the apostrophe are capitalized:

O'Brien	O'Malley

When the particle *Mc* or *Mac* forms part of a name, its first letter is capitalized. Capitalization and spacing of the letters that follow may differ and individual preferences should be respected:

McDonald **or** MacDonald **or** Mac Donald **or** Macdonald

McMillan **or** MacMillan **or** Mac Millan **or** Macmillan

Individual preferences regarding the capitalization and spacing of articles and particles in French names or those of foreign origin should also be respected when they can be ascertained.[1] The following, for example, are correct forms:

Robert de Cotret	Walter de la Mare
Pierre De Bané	Arthur Vandenberg
John Dos Passos	Cornelius Van Horne

In the case of historical figures, treatment in English may differ from that in the original language, and no real standard appears to exist. Consistency in treating a particular name (such as *Leonardo da Vinci, Luca della Robbia* or *Vincent van Gogh*) is all that can be aimed for. In some cases, the most familiar form of the name omits the particle entirely:

Beethoven (Ludwig van Beethoven)

Torquemada (Tomas de Torquemada)

4.04 Words derived from proper nouns

As a general rule, capitalize an adjective derived from a proper noun or composed of a proper name:

Canadian whisky	Franciscan friar
Digby chicken	Newtonian physics

Proper adjectives are associated with the person or place from whose name they are derived. When this association is remote, the adjective becomes common and in most cases no longer takes a capital, as illustrated below:

bohemian lifestyle	manila envelope
chinaware	platonic relationship

In the same way, verbs derived from proper nouns are capitalized unless their association with the proper noun is remote:

Anglicize

Frenchify

but

italicize

vulcanize

It is important to check proper noun derivatives carefully, however. Usage in this regard is not standardized.

---

1. *Anglo-American Cataloguing Rules*, p. 348-93, is an excellent source of such information.

4.05 Governments and government bodies

Capitalize the titles of governments and government departments and agencies, their organizational subdivisions at all levels, the names of boards and committees, and *the Crown* when it means the supreme governing authority:

> the Government of Canada (the Government)
> the Parliament of Canada (Parliament)
> the House of Commons (the House)
> the Senate of Canada (the Senate)
> the Public Service Commission (the Commission)
> the Department of Labour (the Department)
> the Public Affairs Section (the Section)
> the Management Committee (the Committee)

Note that both the legal title and the applied title of a federal department are capitalized:

> the Department of Labour   Labour Canada

When the short forms shown in parentheses above are used after the full titles have been given, they too should be capitalized. However, when used in a non-specific sense, when preceded by a possessive, demonstrative or other type of adjective, and when used adjectivally or in an adjectival form, they are normally written in lower case:

> We have formed a committee to study the matter.
> Our section held its monthly meeting yesterday.
> This division has 60 employees.
> The Canadian (federal, Conservative, present) government
> has issued a policy statement.
> An interpretation of the departmental rules and regulations
> is required.
> The question of parliamentary procedure was raised.
> Unfortunately, division practice proscribes such an approach.

Exceptions:
If the short title is a specific term which the organization shares with no other body within the government concerned, that title retains the upper case when used adjectivally:

> the question of Senate reform
> some House committees

Do not capitalize the plural forms of *government, department, division,* etc., even when the full titles of the bodies concerned are given:

> Representatives from the departments of Finance, External
> Affairs, and Energy, Mines and Resources were present.
> The governments of Canada and France took a similar
> position on the issue.

4.06 Institutions

Capitalize the official names of organized churches, universities, school boards, schools, courts of law, clubs, corporations, associations, political parties, etc.:

the Carleton School Board
Lisgar Collegiate Institute
the Supreme Court
    of Canada
the Quebec Superior Court
the International Court
    of Justice
the First Baptist Church
but a Baptist church

the Rotary Club
the Bell Telephone Company
the Canadian Medical
    Association
the New Democratic Party
the University of Manitoba
the Opposition (official)

Note:

The rules given in 4.05 for short titles are also applicable here.

Capitalize adjectives and nouns referring to the ideas, actions and members of specific political parties:

a Conservative policy paper (of the Conservative government
or Party)
Liberals (members of the Liberal Party)

but

the liberal arts
a conservative on moral issues

4.07 Official documents

Capitalize the names of treaties, agreements, pieces of legislation and other official documents:

the Treaty of Versailles
the Financial Administration Act
the White Paper on Taxation
Order-in-Council P.C. 1354

Capitalize *Addendum, Comment, Communication, Letter, Note* and *Circular* in first references when they are used as the title of a specific document or section of a document.

4.08   Titles of office or rank

Capitalize civil, military, religious and professional titles and titles of nobility when they precede a personal name:

Queen Elizabeth II	Professor Layton
Lord Carrington	General Thériault
Prime Minister Mulroney	President Reagan
Finance Minister	Cardinal Carter
Michael Wilson	

Capitalize all titles following and placed in apposition to a personal name, except those denoting professions:

Clare Smith, Director of Public Affairs
John Crosbie, Minister of Justice

but

Jane Tanaka, professor of physics

Capitalize titles given in full without a personal name:

the Secretary of State for External Affairs
the Dean of Arts
the Chief, Public Affairs Section
the Leader of the Opposition

Do not capitalize them when they are in the plural or are preceded by an indefinite article:

the lieutenant-governors of Quebec and Ontario
a member of Parliament **but**
the Member for Winnipeg North Centre

Capitalize a title referring to a specific person and used as a substitute for the person's name and as a short form of the full title:

They discussed the matter with the Colonel.
The Archbishop made no further comment.

Titles are lower-cased when modified by a possessive or other type of adjective:

They discussed it with their colonel.
They discussed it with the former ambassador.
They discussed it with the Canadian prime minister.

In cases such as these, as well as those cited under 4.05, 4.06 and 4.07, much depends on the context and the target readership. One style (with capitals used freely) would be appropriate for an "in-house" readership and another (a "down" style) for outsiders. The style chosen depends on the degree of importance and amount of respect the reader may be expected to accord the person, position or institution in question.

Titles of respect and forms of address are capitalized in any context, even when used in the plural:

Your Excellency	Mr. Chairman
Your Honour	Their Royal Highnesses
Your Grace	Her Worship

4.09 Family appellations

Capitalize family appellations only when the name of a person follows, when they are unmodified, or when they are used in direct address:

Grandmother Smith
Aunt Sarah
I met Mother at the theatre.
Tell me, Son, where you have been.

but

John's grandmother
my aunt

4.10 Races, languages and peoples

Capitalize nouns and adjectives denoting race, tribe, nationality and language:

Caucasian	Indian
Inuk (plural: Inuit)	Francophone
Métis	Anglophone
Amerindian	Arabic
Cree	French

The form of some words may vary depending on the meaning:

Highlander (inhabitant of the Scottish Highlands)
highlander (inhabitant of any highland area)
Aborigine (one of the indigenous peoples of Australia)
aborigine (indigenous inhabitant of a region)
Pygmy (member of a group of African peoples)
pygmy (small in stature; insignificant)

Note that the terms *native people(s)* and *aboriginal people(s)* are lower-cased.

4.11 School subjects, courses and degrees

In keeping with 4.10 above, the names of languages are always capitalized. Do not capitalize the names of other disciplines when used in a general sense. When used to refer to school subjects or the names of particular courses, they should be capitalized:

> She is interested in history.
> He reads articles on economics and biology in his spare time.

> **but**

> She passed with a "B" in History this term.
> He is taking Chemistry 101 and Economics 406.

Do not capitalize the name of a degree in general references, but do capitalize it when it follows a person's name and when its title is stated in full:

> Janet is earning her master's degree.
> Ellen Compton, Doctor of Philosophy
> He holds a Master of Arts degree from McGill University.

4.12 Military terms

Capitalize the names of military bases, forces and units of all sizes and of decorations, medals and exercises:[2]

the Canadian Forces	450 Helicopter Squadron
Mobile Command	Exercise Rapier Thrust
Canadian Forces Base Trenton	the Victoria Cross

4.13 Ships, aircraft, etc.

Capitalize the names of types of aircraft, the names of makes of cars and other modes of transportation, and the names of individual ships, locomotives, spacecraft, etc.:

> the Cessna-7
> a Boeing 747
> HMCS *Donnacona* (italics for the name; roman type for the designation abbreviation)
> the Bricklin
> *Mariner IV*

See 6.07 for further information about the italicization of such names.

---

2. In Canadian Forces writing, the names of exercises and vessels are written in full capitals.

4.14 Time references

Capitalize the names of months and days, of holidays and holy days, of historical and geological periods and events, and of parliamentary sessions:

Wednesday	the Ice Age
October	the Second World War
Thanksgiving Day	World War II
April Fools' Day	the Middle Ages
Passover	the Six-Day War
Christmas	the Pleistocene era
The First Session of the	
Thirty-second Parliament	

Do not capitalize the names of the seasons, centuries or decades unless they are personified or are part of special names:

spring
winter
the twentieth century
the fifties

but

the Roaring Twenties (name of an era)
the Winter Palace

4.15 Cultural periods, movements and styles

Capitalize nouns and adjectives designating literary, philosophical, musical, religious and artistic periods, movements and styles when they are derived from proper names:

Aristotelian logic	Romanesque architecture
Cartesian dualism	Arianism
the Bauhaus	Methodism
Gregorian chant	Hasidism

Otherwise, such terms are lower-cased except when it is necessary to distinguish a style or movement from the same word used in the general sense. Thus:

cubism	the New Criticism
existentialism	the Group of Seven
humanism	the Enlightenment
rococo	Scholasticism

4.16 Deities

Capitalize names, synonyms and personifications of deities:

God	Siva
the Creator	Zeus
the Almighty	Woden
Mother Nature	Allah
Jehovah	Manitou

Capitalize personal pronouns referring to God, but not relative pronouns:

Trust in Him whose strength will uphold you.

4.17 Religious denominations

Capitalize the names of religious denominations, sects and orders, as well as adjectives and verbs derived from them which relate to religion:

Anglican	the Dominican order
Roman Catholic	Buddhism
Greek Orthodox	Jehovah's Witnesses
Christianize	Shiite

but

She is very catholic in her literary tastes.
His ideas are quite orthodox.

4.18 Religious documents

Capitalize the titles of religious writings and documents:

the Bible	the Koran
Deuteronomy	the Torah
the Dead Sea Scrolls	the Ten Commandments

4.19 Religious events

Capitalize the names of events recorded in sacred writings and of historical events with a strong religious dimension:

the Flood	the Reformation
the Exodus	the Crusades
the Crucifixion	the Great Schism
the Hegira	the Immaculate Conception

4.20 Geographical terms

Capitalize the names of countries, regions, counties, cities and other official and specified political, administrative and geographical divisions and topographical features:

Canada	the Grassy Narrows Reserve
the Northern Hemisphere	the Pacific
the International Boundary	Alberta
the Prairies	Lanark County
the Canadian Shield	Sherbrooke
the Maritimes	Pickle Lake
the Atlantic provinces	Elm Street West
the Ontario Region (sector	the Okanagan Valley
of government department)	the South Saskatchewan River
the Atlantic provinces	the Crow's Nest Pass

A generic term such as *city, county, state* or *province* is lower-cased when it precedes the proper name or stands alone, unless it is used in a corporate sense:

the city of Toronto
the county of Lanark
the province of Nova Scotia
the state of New York

but

Province of Ontario bonds
Smith v. The State of New York

Do not capitalize a generic term used in the plural:

lakes Huron and Ontario
the Thompson and Fraser rivers

In general, do not capitalize the names of compass points or similar descriptive terms unless they have taken on political or other connotations or form the titles of administrative regions:

northern New Brunswick
the west of Saskatchewan

but

the West
Western values
East European countries
the Far East
the Far North
the Eastern Townships
Northern Ontario

4.21 Buildings, monuments and public places

Capitalize the official names of specific buildings, monuments, squares, parks, etc.:

the National Gallery

the Peace Bridge

the Plains of Abraham

the Toronto Public Library

the Vancouver International
   Airport **but** the Vancouver airport

Robson Square

the O'Keefe Centre

the Brock Monument

St. Andrew's Church

4.22 Astronomical terms

Capitalize the names of planets and other astronomical bodies and configurations. But capitalize *earth, sun* and *moon* only when they are referred to in relation to other planets or heavenly bodies:

Venus

the Great Bear

The sun shines bright.

Mercury is closer than the Earth to the Sun.

4.23 Biological classification

Capitalize the scientific name of a phylum, order, class, family or genus, but not common names or the epithets referring to a species or subspecies:

the phylum Arthropoda

the order Rosales

the genus *Sporotrichum*

the species *Sporotrichum schenkii*
   (second word denotes species)

The jaguar and the lion are members of the family Felidae.

See 6.11 for rules governing the italicization of biological classifications.

Capitalize a proper noun modifying a common name:

Grayson lily

Queen Anne's lace

Cupid's-delight

Judas tree

4.24 Trade names

Capitalize trade names of drugs and any other manufactured products unless they have become established as common nouns. To determine this, check the *Canadian Trade Index* or your dictionary:

Plexiglas

Valium

Kleenex

Anacin

but

cellophane
nylon
aspirin

Note:
Where possible, avoid the use of trade names as generic nouns or adjectives.
For example, write *adhesive tape*, not *Scotch tape*.

4.25 Scientific names with eponyms

In scientific terms composed of a common noun preceded by a proper noun,
an adjective derived from a proper noun or by a proper noun with an apostrophe
s, capitalize the adjective or proper noun but not the common noun. Do not
capitalize the names of laws or theories or the names of minerals, particles
or elements derived from proper names:

Hodgkin's disease	Becquerel rays
Reiter's syndrome	Gaussian curve
Bohr radius	Ohm's law

but

the general theory of relativity
the second law of thermodynamics
forsterite
boson
germanium

Note that certain personal names begin with a small letter:

van't Hoff equation
van Willebrand disease

4.26 Metric and SI units

Capitalize only the word *Celsius* when writing the names of metric and SI
units in full. When using symbols, capitalize all those based on proper nouns
and the letter *L* for *litre:*

30 m (metres)	12 000 Hz (hertz)
475 g (grams)	30 L (litres)

Capitalize the symbols for the prefixes from *mega* to *exa.* The symbols for
the others remain in lower case. Consistency is important here because the
letters *m* and *p* are both used in symbols for two different prefixes:

mg (milligram)	Mg (megagram)
pm (picometre)	Pm (petametre)

See also 1.22.

4.27 Computer languages

The names of computer languages should be fully capitalized:

FORTRAN	COBOL
BASIC	ALGOL

See 1.16 for information about capitalizing other types of acronyms and initialisms.

4.28 Books, articles, plays, musical compositions, etc.

In English titles of books, articles, periodicals, newspapers, plays, musical works and recordings, poems, paintings, sculptures and motion pictures, capitalize all words except articles, conjunctions, prepositions and the *to* in infinitives. These exceptions are also capitalized when they immediately follow a period, colon or dash within a title and when they are the first or last word in a title:

(book)	*Virginia Woolf: A Biography*
(book)	*Under the Volcano*
(play)	*How to Succeed in Business without Really Trying*
(painting)	*Rain in the North Country*
(film)	*Goin' down the Road*

In titles containing hyphenated compounds, always capitalize the first element. Capitalize the second element if it is a proper noun or proper adjective or if it is as important as the first element:

A History of Eighteenth-Century Literature
Neo-Colonialism in Africa
Anti-Americanism in Latin America

Do not capitalize the second element if it is simply a modifier of the first, or if the hyphenated elements constitute a single word:

Sonata in E-flat Major
Co-operation for Development

4.29 The definite article

Capitalize *the* when it is part of a corporate name:

The Globe and Mail	The Pas

The French definite article should be retained if it is part of a corporate name, and *the* should not precede it. If the French article is not part of the official title, replace it with *the:*

an article in *Le Devoir*

but

a representative of the Office de la langue française

4.30 The salutation and complimentary close

Use capitals for the first word and all nouns in the salutation of a letter, but only for the first word in a close:

My dear Sir	Yours truly
Dear Madam	Very sincerely yours

4.31 Hyphenated compounds

A proper noun or adjective in a hyphenated compound retains the capital:

Greco-Roman	neo-Nazi
trans-Canada	Pan-American

Usage varies in the case of full compounds:

transatlantic

transpacific

but

ClearTerm

TriStar

4.32 Legal usage

In legal writing some common nouns referring to parties to an action, the names of documents or judicial bodies are capitalized:

Counsel for the Plaintiff

The Court (*meaning* the judge) sustained the objection.

the said Notary

the aforementioned Agreement

but

The court was in session.

4.33 Parts of a book or document

Capitalize certain common nouns in the singular when they are used in text references with numbers or letters indicating place, position or major division in a sequence. A letter following such a term is also capitalized:

Act ii	Figure vii
Appendix B	Plate iv
Chapter 3	Scene iii
Chart 2	Table iii
Corollary 1	Theorem 3
Exhibit A	Volume 13

Minor subdivisions such as *page, note, line, paragraph* and *verse* are written in lower case:

> See page 6, line 48.

Note that *section*, when used for part of a law or set of regulations, is not capitalized; however, if it refers to a large subdivision of a report, book or other document, it is capitalized:

> under section 23 of the Act
> Volume 10, Section 5

4.34 Single letters used as words

Capitalize a single letter used as a word, whether hyphenated or not:

C minor	U-turn
H-bomb	vitamin A
T-shirt	X-ray

Five

Numerical expressions

5

Numerical expressions

5.01 Introduction

Numerical information should be conveyed in such a way as to be comprehended quickly, easily and without ambiguity. For this reason, figures are preferred to spelled-out forms in technical writing. Except in certain adjectival expressions (see 5.05) and in technical writing, write out one-digit numbers and use figures for the rest. Ordinals should be treated in the same way as cardinal numbers, e.g. *seven* and *seventh, 101* and *101st.*

Many other factors enter into the decision whether to write numbers out or to express them in figures. This chapter will discuss the most important of these and present some of the conventions governing the use of special signs and symbols with figures. The rules stated should, in most cases, be regarded as guidelines for general use which may be superseded by the requirements of particular applications.

5.02 Round numbers

Write out numbers used figuratively:

a thousand and one excuses

They may attack me with an army of six hundred syllogisms.
—Erasmus

And torture one poor word ten thousand ways.
—Dryden

Numbers in the millions or higher that require more than two words may be written as a combination of words and figures:

23 million   3.1 million

There were more than 2.5 million Canadians between the ages of 30 and 40 in 1971.

When such compound numbers are used adjectivally, insert hyphens between the components (see 5.05):

a 1.7-million increase in population

Whether or not it is used adjectivally, the entire number (numeral and word) should appear on the same line.

Numbers with a long succession of zeros should normally be rewritten. Thus *2.6 million* is preferable to *2 600 000*.

Numbers are normally rounded to no more than three significant digits. Thus *2 653 000* becomes *2.65 million,* not *2.653 million.*

The proper form for large numbers that must be written in full is as illustrated:

one hundred and fifty-two thousand three hundred and five

Only in legal documents should a number which is written in full be repeated in figures in parentheses:

nineteen hundred and eighty-four (1984)

5.03   Consistency

Numbers modifying the same items should be treated alike within a given passage. If figures are to be used for any, they should be used for all the numbers of those items:

Of the 318 outlets established in these five provinces over the past eight years, only 6 accept more than two major credit cards.

Out of a population of 74 000 000, only 360 000 voted for the Socialist candidate.

the 3rd, 6th and 127th items in the series

Where many numbers occur in close succession, express all of them in figures, especially in statistical matter.

5.04   Initial numbers

Spell out a number—or the word *number*—when it occurs at the beginning of a sentence, as well as any related numbers which closely follow it:

Three hundred persons were expected, but only twenty-three showed up.

Number 6 was the last in the series; there was no number 7.

Where this would result in a cumbersome construction, it may be necessary to recast the sentence. The first sentence above could be rewritten as

A crowd of 300 was expected, but only 23 showed up.

To avoid starting with a number, it may be possible to end the preceding sentence with a semicolon or to punctuate in some other manner. Instead of writing

But that was now in the past. 1984 was another year.

you could insert a semicolon after *past* or write "... in the past, and 1984. ..."

In accordance with 5.10, a number followed by a unit of measurement may have to be written in figures. Thus

18.3 cm/s was the best result we could obtain.

should be rewritten as

A result of 18.3 cm/s was the best we could obtain.

not

Eighteen point three. . . .

5.05 Adjectival expressions and juxtaposed numbers

Normally, for numbers used in adjectival expressions, follow the rule given in 5.01, i.e. write out those from one to nine and use figures for the rest:

seven-hour day
two-metre-wide entrance
a 10-year-old boy

If the unit is represented by an abbreviation or symbol, use figures (see 1.22):

a 2.36 m high jump
three 5-L containers

or

three 5 L containers

Do not use a hyphen between a figure and a non-letter symbol:

a 90° angle
four 100°C thermometers

When a number immediately precedes a compound modifier containing another number, spell out the first or the smaller number:

ten 34-cent stamps	75 10-cent stamps
two 10-room houses	120 eight-page reports

5.06 Mathematical usage

Numbers treated as nouns in mathematical usage should always be given in figures:

multiply by 3	a factor of 2	14 plus 6

Algebraic expressions used in association with units of measurement should be distinguished from the latter by means of italics, unless the units are written in full:

$3ab$ metres   **or** $3ab$ m

5.07 Ratios

The usual forms are:

> 1 to 4 **or** 1:4
> 1:3:4 (1 to 3 to 4)
> 3:19::12:76 (3 is to 19 as 12 is to 76)

Certain types of ratios may be re-expressed as percentages or decimals. For example, *a slope of 1:10* may be written as *a 10% slope*.

5.08 Fractions

In non-technical writing, spell out simple fractions, especially when used in isolation:

> half of one per cent
>
> half an inch
>
> **or**
>
> one-half inch
>
> a quarter of an inch
>
> **or**
>
> one-quarter inch
>
> three quarters of an inch
>
> **or**
>
> three-quarters inch (**not** inches)
>
> three-quarter length

When a fraction is used adjectivally, place a hyphen between the numerator and the denominator unless either of these elements is itself hyphenated:

> four-fifths inch
> six thirty-seconds
> twenty five-thousandths
> twenty-five thousandths

Fractions such as the last two, which lend themselves to confusion, are better expressed in figures.

It is incorrect to use *th* or *ths* after fractions expressed in figures:

> 1/25 **not** 1/25th
>
> 3/100 **not** 3/100ths

A fraction expressed in figures should not be followed by *of a* or *of an:*

> 3/8 inch **not** 3/8 of an inch

If the sentence seems to require *of a*, the fraction should be spelled out.

Mixed numbers (combinations of a whole number and a fraction) should be given in figures:

2¾ **but** time and a half for overtime

5.09 Decimal fractions

In technical and statistical writing and with metric and SI units, decimals are preferred to fractions. Normally, no number should begin or end with a decimal point. A zero is written before the decimal point of numbers smaller than 1, while in whole numbers the decimal point should either be absent or be followed by a zero:

| $0.64 | **not** | $.64 |
| 11 **or** 11.0 | **not** | 11. |

Exceptions:

a .39 calibre revolver

.999 fine gold

See also 5.16.

Zeros may be used to indicate the number of decimal places to which a value is significant: *0.60* implies significance to two decimal places, *0.600* to three.

Note 1:
In many countries the decimal marker is the comma, not the period. The Metric Commission, however, recommends the use of the period as the decimal marker in English-language texts in Canada. Writers and editors should be aware that both methods of indicating the decimal are in current use and are appropriate, depending on the context.

Note 2:
Formerly, groups of three figures were separated from one another by a comma in the English-speaking world. To prevent such a comma from being mistaken for the decimal marker used by most countries and to comply with the decisions of the Metric Commission and International Standard ISO 31/0, it is recommended that this practice be abandoned except in financial documents.[1] A space should be used instead of a comma, and such a space is also to be inserted after groups of three digits to the right of a decimal point. Note that numbers of four digits only (on either side of the decimal marker) need not be so spaced unless used in combination with other numbers of more than four digits. The following examples illustrate the correct use of the space to separate triads of numbers:

whole numbers	decimals
5005 **or** 5 005	5.0005 **or** 5.000 5
50 005	5.000 05
500 005	5.000 005
500 005 000	5.000 005 000

1. It is currently the policy of the Government of Canada to continue to use the comma to separate triads of numbers on payment instruments and financial documents. This policy, which is consistent with that accepted by the Canadian Bankers' Association, is stated in Treasury Board Circular No. 1979-7 (April 9, 1979) and clarified in TB Circular No. 1984-64 (November 7, 1984).

Omit the space in pagination, inclusive numbers, addresses, numbering of verse, telephone numbers, library numbers, serial numbers and the like.[2]

5.10 Quantities and measures

When quantities or measures consist of two or more elements, when they are used in a technical context, or when a decimal marker is involved, write them in figures. Otherwise, follow the rule of writing the number out if it is less than 10 (see 5.01):

> three miles
> 5.6 km
> 20/20 vision
> a magnification of 50 **or** a 50X magnification
> one metre equals approximately 39 inches
> two metres tall
> 1.6 m tall **not** 1 m 60 cm tall
> six feet tall
> 5 feet 11 inches tall (no comma between elements)
> 8½ by 11 inch paper **or** 8½ x 11 inch paper
> 50 cm x 75 cm x 2 m (unit repeated to avoid ambiguity)

Use of the International System of units (SI units) is now mandatory in technical writing, with certain exceptions. In particular, its use in Canada is required by the Metric Commission. Basic information about SI symbols and their use is found in Chapter 1 of this guide. For more detailed information, consult the *Metric Editorial Handbook* published by the Canadian Standards Association (CSA Publication Z372-1980), the *Canadian Metric Practice Guide* (CAN3-Z234.1-79) or the *Metric Press Guide* of Metric Commission Canada. The following are some salient points relating particularly to the use of figures:

• As noted in 1.22, SI usage requires either that both the figure and the unit be written in full or that both be abbreviated:

> two metres **or** 2 m
> **not**
> 2 metres **or** two m

• Prefixed units should not normally appear as denominators in expressions of the form g/cm^3, which should be re-expressed in terms of cubic metres.

An exception to this rule is the symbol *kg,* since the kilogram is considered the base unit of mass.

---

2. See *Metric Editorial Handbook,* p. 25, for examples.

- When one type of unit is converted to another in non-technical work, the converted value should normally be rounded to within five percent of the initial figure and should be preceded by the word *about* or some other indication that the value is an approximation:

> 5 lb. or about 2.3 kg

The following conventions for using the degree symbol should be noted:

> 40°   40 proof
> 30°−50° (symbol repeated) **but** 30±2°C
> 10−15°C
> −10 to −15°C **not** −10−15°C
> 10°C   10.5°C
> 300 K **not** 300°K
> 10° (of arc)
> 10.5° **or** 10°5 **or** 10°30′ **or** 10°30′00″
> 36°N lat.   36th parallel
> mm/degree **not** mm/° (° not to be used alone in denominator)

Percent is usually written out in non-technical material, except when used adjectivally:

> 15 percent   a 15% bond (no space between numeral and %)

5.11   Money

Sums of money are usually expressed in figures, except when they refer to round or indefinite amounts or are used in a formal or legal context:

> $5.98 per m²   a few thousand dollars
> a fare of 75¢   a twenty-dollar bill
>
> Payments shall be made in equal instalments of two hundred and thirty dollars per month.

The following forms should be used:

> 65¢ **or** $0.65 **or** 65 cents **not** $.65 **or** .65¢
> two million dollars **or** $2 million **or** $2 000 000
> **or** $2,000,000[3]
> a two-million dollar loan (see 5.05)
> $100 **not** $100. **or** $100.00 (when standing alone)
> five dollars **or** $5 **not** 5 dollars
> $5 worth **not** $5′ worth

---

3. See 5.09, note 2.

The abbreviations *M* for *million*, *m* or *G* for *thousand* and *c* for *hundred*, sometimes seen with figures, lend themselves to confusion with metric symbols and should therefore be avoided. *K* for *thousand* is acceptable in internal documents.

When dollar amounts are used with metric symbols, the following forms are required:

$11.50/m² **not** $11.50/square metre

$3.99/kg **not** $3.99/kilogram **or** $3.99/kilo

98¢/L **or** 98¢ per litre **not** 0.98¢ per litre

The dollar sign should be placed before the figure in question.

For methods of indicating dollar amounts in Canadian and other currencies, see 5.26.

5.12 Representation of time in ordinary prose and with SI units

In ordinary prose, times of day are usually spelled out, especially when they are approximate:

The meeting was called to order at ten o'clock.

His appointment was scheduled for two-thirty.

When exact time is to be emphasized, however, figures are used:

The program will be broadcast at 8:05 p.m.

The train leaves at 6:20 a.m.

Note that precise measurements of duration given in a scientific or technical context should be expressed by means of the internationally recognized symbols of time *d* for day, *h* for *hour,* *min* for *minute* and *s* for *second:*

7 h 20 min flying time

The test run took 1 d 3 h 43 min 09 s precisely.

These symbols should also be used when units of time are expressed with SI units:

16 km/d	16 m/s
10 J/h	60 r/min

5.13 Representation of time of day

In documents presented in both official languages, and in all forms of international communication, it may be desirable to use the 24-hour system for representing time of day, in accordance with International Standard ISO 3307 and the Treasury Board *Design Guide.*[4]

---

4. Treasury Board of Canada, Federal Identity Program, *Design Guide,* Appendix A.

The hour is represented by a two-digit number ranging from 00 up to 23 (or 24), the minute and second are represented by a two-digit number ranging from 00 up to 59, and the colon is used as a separator between hour and minute and between minute and second, as illustrated:

24-hour representation

with seconds	without seconds
00:15:00	00:15
08:00:00	08:00
20:00:00	20:00
12:00:00	12:00
07:15:00	07:15
11:37:00	11:37
14:12:26	14:12

Note:

The instant of midnight should be represented (when seconds are included) as either 24:00:00, the end of one day, or 00:00:00, the beginning of the next day, according to circumstances.

5.14 Dates

For calendar dates, the common alphanumeric method remains acceptable, provided that cardinal numbers are used:

March 15, 1986 **or**   15 March 1986

not

March 15th, 1986 **or**   March fifteenth, 1986

When the day and month only are given, ordinal forms may be used:

the 17th of August

or

the seventeenth of August

but not

August 17th

For the use of the comma in dates, see 7.21.

The all-numeric form of dating may be more appropriate for such purposes as office memorandums and chronological files and on documents such as certificates, forms and plaques which are presented in both official languages. The format prescribed below is in accordance with the Treasury Board *Design Guide,* CSA Standard CAN 3-Z234.4-79 and International Standard ISO 2014. The year, month and day should be separated by a space or short dash, as illustrated:

1986 03 27 **or**   1986-03-27 (March 27, 1986)
1987 11 02 **or**   1987-11-02 (November 2, 1987)

The advantage of international standardization in this format is that, whereas *2/11/87* could mean either *November 2, 1987* or *February 11, 1987,* the form *1987-11-02* can mean only the former.

Dates are sometimes spelled out in cases such as the following:

> the Fourth of July
> during the seventies
> He returned on August ninth (reported speech)
> I last saw him on July 4. By the morning of the
> fifth he was dead.

Dates are spelled out in legal texts and in formal invitations and announcements:

> Mr. and Mrs. Walter and Mary Chute
> are pleased to announce
> the marriage of their daughter
> Janet Elizabeth
> to
> Doctor Donald Eric MacLeod
> Saturday the ninth of October
> nineteen hundred and eighty-six

Year designations take the following forms:

> the class of '68
> the 1880s
> 1300 BC
> AD 1300

5.15   Age

Exact age is usually indicated in figures, even if less than 10:

> John, aged 9, and his brother Tom, 10, led the hike.

It is written out, however, in the case of approximate age and in formal contexts:

> He's eighty if he's a day.
> She was no more than seventeen at the time.
> On the occasion of her retirement at the age of sixty-five

5.16   Market quotations

Market quotations are invariably given in figures:

> wheat at 2.30
> sugar, .05 **or** sugar, 0.05
> Preferred stocks sell at 245.
> Fastbuck Fortunes 5s at 17¼

5.17 Votes, scores, etc.

Give votes, scores and odds in figures:

The vote was 51 to 3, with 6 abstentions.
The justices ruled 5 to 3 in his favour.
The Flames beat the Canucks 3 to 2 in overtime.

5.18 Governmental, military and historical designations

a) Write out numbers of dynasties, governing bodies, and sessions of Parliament or Congress as ordinals:

First International	Twenty-fourth Dynasty
Third Reich	Thirty-second Parliament
Fifth Republic	Ninety-seventh Congress

b) Write out ordinal numbers below 100 designating political and administrative divisions:

Fifth Ward	Twenty-second District
Tenth Circuit Court	Fifteenth Precinct

c) Designations of large military units, especially in a foreign or historical context, may be written out in ordinals; otherwise use cardinal figures:

Sixth Fleet	First Canadian Army
5 Combat	422 Tactical
Engineer Regiment	Helicopter Squadron

d) Write out numbers in historical, biblical or formal references:

the Thirteen Colonies	the Twelve Apostles
the Ten Commandments	Twelfth-night

5.19 Names of organizations

Ordinals modifying the names of churches and religious bodies are usually written out:

First Baptist Church
Seventh-Day Adventists
First Church of Christ Scientist

Use Arabic figures in referring to union locals, fraternal lodges and similar organizations:

Teamsters Union Local 91
Loyal Order of Moose 1765
Royal Canadian Legion, Stittsville Branch 618

5.20 Numbers used as nouns

Figures are always used when numbers are referred to as nouns:

> Highway 3
> Channel 3
> Grade 4
> Bulletin No. 40
> Revolution No. 9
> values of 0 and 1
> Engine No. 9 is arriving on Track 3.
> Eastern Provincial Airways Flight 67 now boarding at Gate 6.

5.21 Addresses

Street and avenue designations up to and including *Tenth* are usually spelled out, especially when this helps to prevent confusion with the building number. If the street number is written in figures, modern usage tends to favour cardinal rather than ordinal numbers:

> 9511 Tenth Avenue   96 Ave. and 101 St.

In abbreviated form, apartment or suite numbers are written before the building number and are often followed by a dash:

> 107-6807 92 Ave. N.

Ordinal figures are normally used to identify floors of a building:

> 11th floor, L'Esplanade Laurier

5.22 Reference numbers

Page numbers are often written in Arabic numerals, but in prefatory material they may be written as lower-case Roman numerals:

> page vii of the Foreword
> page 7 of the Introduction

Within the body of the text, volume numbers may be indicated by Arabic or Roman numerals or be spelled out. Numbers of chapters and other major divisions of a book may be spelled out, but are more often written in Roman or Arabic numerals—the tendency being away from Roman numerals in the case of both chapter and volume numbers. Verse numbers and those of minor divisions of a book are written as Arabic numerals:

> I Kings 9:1–4
> Volume 18, Section 8

Paragraphs may be numbered 1,2, . . .; clauses within paragraphs, 1), 2),. . . . Groups of paragraphs may be numbered with Roman numerals. In citations from legislation and the like, section and subsection numbers should be enclosed in parentheses with no space between them:

> section 123(4)(*b*)(ii)

5.23 Plurals

Plurals of figures are usually formed by adding an *s:*

the 1960s   five 55s
The bonds are 4½ s.
Korolev scored 9.85s on the floor and pommel horse exercises.

In cases where this might cause misreading, an apostrophe and *s* should be added or the figure italicized:

6's and 7's **or** 6s and 7s

Whichever practice is adopted, consistency should be maintained in any one document.

Do not pluralize metric and SI unit symbols:

5 kg   **not**   5 kgs

5.24 Comparative and inclusive numbers

a) For general comparisons note the following:

five times as great   **not**   five times greater
one fifth as large   **not**   five times smaller

Note that "a four-to-one margin" is meaningless; "a margin of three" is correct.

Note the difference between:

   i) increased by 10 to 15% (e.g. from 20 to 22 or 23)
  ii) increased by 10% to 15% (i.e. from 5%)
 iii) increased from 10% to 15% (i.e. by 5%)
 iv) increased from 10 to 15% (same as iii)

b) Consecutive numbers are joined by *or* or *and*, except where intermediate quantities are possible:

Five or six apples
rows 5 and 6
but
a range of 5 to 6
rather than
5 or 6

In references to successive pages, *p. 15, 16* indicates matter which is disconnected in the two pages, while *p. 15-16* indicates that the subject is continuous from the first page to the second.

c) Opinions differ on the proper forms for inclusive numbers written as figures. To ensure clarity, abbreviate second numbers according to the following principles.

Repeat all digits in numbers below 100:

4−10   67−68   82−99

Repeat all digits where the first number is 100 or a multiple of 100:

100−138   700−706   1900−1901

Where the first number is in the range 101−109, in multiples of 100, use the changed part only and omit unnecessary zeros:

103−9   808−18   1007−8

Where the first number is in the range 110−199, in multiples of 100, use two or more digits, as needed:

435−37   1986−87   3740−75

With numbers of four digits, use all digits if three of them change:

1889−1915

Note the following special cases:

899−900 (second digit with even hundred)
398−396 BC (all digits repeated in years BC)

5.25 Roman numerals

Roman numerals are becoming increasingly rare, but they still have the following uses:

• names of rulers, aristocrats, and the names of ships, racing cars and space vehicles:

Charles IV   *Bluenose* II
Pius XII   *Mariner* IV

• numbers of volumes, chapters, tables, plates, acts and other divisions of a book or play (now often replaced by Arabic numerals):

Psalm XXIII
Volume XII
Appendix III
Act II, Scene iii (act number in upper case, scene number
  in lower case)
Iliad xi.26

• years, centuries and recurring events of major importance:

MCMLXXXVI (in very formal contexts)
XIX Century
XX Olympiad

99

Do not use ordinal forms (*st, nd, th,* etc.) with Roman numerals.

Lower-case Roman numerals may be used for prefatory pagination, subclauses and subordinate classifications in a series.

Note that a bar over a letter in a Roman numeral multiplies its value by 1000:

$$\overline{D} = 500\ 000 \qquad\qquad \overline{V} = 5\ 000$$

5.26   Other considerations

Clarity should be the primary consideration when communicating numerical information. Present it in such a way that it will be readily grasped by the reader. When writing for non-Canadians, make sure you are aware of the conventions used in the target country. Europeans, for example, who are steeped in the metric system, do not confine themselves as we usually do to multiples of 1000. They will more naturally write *3 dL* (decilitres) than *300 mL* or *0.3 L*. Material written for the European market will appear more natural if it conforms to this practice.

Remember, too, that in Europe—and in Quebec—*1,500* means "one and a half", and *1.500* means "fifteen hundred." The British "billion" is the equivalent of the American "trillion," while a British "trillion" is a million million million. In certain circumstances it may be advisable to write a *thousand million* or *10⁹* or *giga-* instead of *billion*, and a *million million* or *10¹²* or *tera-* instead of *trillion*, to avoid the risk of misinterpretation. For similar reasons, the abbreviation *ppb* (parts per billion) should not be used. Rewrite *100 ppb* as *0.1 ppm*.

Dollar amounts in different currencies should be distinguished from one another by some easily understood marker. A reference to $20 will be ambiguous to a non-Canadian reader and may be taken to refer to American or some other currency. No single system is universally accepted, but the following is the one used by the Department of Finance and the International Monetary Fund:

C$20   for Canadian dollars
US$20   for American dollars
A$20   for Australian dollars
NZ$20   for New Zealand dollars

If greater clarity is required, the abbreviations *CAN* and *AUS* may be used.

Where the reader may be in doubt as to which conventions should be followed for writing numerical expressions, the safest course is to adhere to international conventions (see 5.09, notes 1 and 2).

Six

Italics

6

Italics

6.01 Introduction

Because italic (sloping) type *contrasts* with roman (vertical) type, a writer can require words or passages to be typeset in italics in order to call special attention to them, to give them special meaning, or to distinguish them from the rest of his or her text.

Where italic type is not available, underlining can be used for the same purpose. In a manuscript to be sent for printing, underline material to be set in italics.

Italics and underlining should be used sparingly, or they lose their effectiveness.

When an entire passage is printed in italics, the punctuation (including parentheses) and any numbers (including footnote references) will also be in italics. If just a word or phrase is in italics, only the punctuation proper to it is printed in that typeface.

Note that when the main body of a text is printed in italics, roman type is used for emphasis and for the other purposes described in this chapter.

6.02 Emphasis

Italics can serve to indicate emphasis in the following cases:

• when the writer uses an unexpected word:

> What differences might we expect to see in human behaviour if honesty were shown to be the *worst* policy?

• when two words are contrasted:

> I did not say we *would* go: I said we *might* go.

• when the writer wishes to stress a word that would not normally be stressed in the sentence:

> Why was *he* chosen to chair the committee?

6.03 French and foreign words and phrases

These are written in italics if they are not yet considered to be Anglicized. Many such terms occur in legal, political and musical contexts:

allegro non troppo	*mutatis mutandis*
caveat emptor	*raison d'état*
con molto sentimento	*res ipsa loquitur*

When a word or phrase has become Anglicized, the use of italics is discontinued:

ad hoc	per capita
aide-de-camp	regime
à la carte	sombrero

Since neither the latest editions of *Webster* nor the *Gage Canadian Dictionary* indicate which words or phrases are to be italicized, consult *The Concise Oxford Dictionary* and exercise your own judgment, with due regard for the type of text and intended readership. When in doubt, use roman type.

If an unfamiliar French or foreign term or phrase is used repeatedly in a text, it should be italicized the first time it is used and should be accompanied by a definition of its meaning and use. Subsequently, it may be set in roman type.

6.04 Latin terms and abbreviations

Although there is a growing tendency to print all Latin reference terms and abbreviations in roman type, the following are usually italicized:

et seq.	*q.v.*
idem	*sic*
infra	*supra*
passim	*vide*

Do not italicize the following:

AD	QED	e.g.	loc. cit.
BC	ca., c.	i.e.	ibid.
NB	cf.	v., vs.	op. cit.
PS	etc.	viz.	et al.

6.05 Titles of works of art and publications

In printed matter, italicize the titles of books, pamphlets, published reports and studies, plays, operas and long musical compositions, paintings, sculptures, novels, films, long poems, newspapers and periodicals:

(book)	*Civil Service Office Manual*
(pamphlet)	*Keeping the Heat In*
(report)	*Public Accounts of Canada*
(play)	*Murder in the Cathedral*
(opera)	*Rigoletto*
(painting)	*Guernica*
(novel)	*Cabbagetown*
(long poem)	*The Rime of the Ancient Mariner*
(sculpture)	*David*
(newspaper)	*The Globe and Mail*
(periodical)	*Saturday Night*

In typewritten material, underline such titles.

Exception: Titles of scientific periodicals are usually abbreviated and set in roman type (see 9.15).

Titles of articles, short poems and short stories, songs, arias and other short musical compositions, and radio and television programs are set in roman type and enclosed in quotation marks:

(article)	"The Life Beyond"
(aria)	"Pace, pace, mio Dio"
(musical composition)	Chopin's "Revolutionary" Etude, Op. 10, No. 12
(television program)	"The Fifth Estate"

6.06 Legal references

In legal texts italicize the names of statutes and court cases:

the *Official Languages Act*
the *Divorce Act*
Weiner v. The Queen
Robson v. Chrysler Corporation

See also 6.10.

6.07 Names of individual ships, etc.

Italicize the names given to individual ships, trains, aircraft and spacecraft, but not abbreviations such as *HMCS* preceding them:

HMCS *Assiniboine*	the *Spirit of St. Louis*
the spacecraft *Challenger*	the *Rapido*

6.08 Letters and words referred to as such

These should be italicized, e.g.:

Delete the second *and* from line 15.
There is only one *s* in *disappoint*.

Quotation marks (see 8.11), boldface type and underlining may perform the same function.

6.09 Peripheral matter in a text

Italics may be used to set off peripheral matter such as prefaces and dedications or epigraphs and quotations at the beginning of a book or chapter. Stage directions for a play are usually set in italics and placed within brackets or parentheses. Introductory matter setting the scene is also usually in italics, but not in brackets or parentheses.

Italicize the terms *See*, *See under*, *See also* and *See also under* when used in indexes, and the expressions *To be continued*, *Continued on p.*, *Continued from p.* and *Continued on next page*.

Italicize editorial clarifications:

Representatives from certain Carribean [*sic*] countries . . .
[*My emphasis*]
[*Translation*]

See 8.10 and 8.14 for further information on this point.

6.10 Identifying matter

Italicize:

• letters referring to subdivisions of a statute or other regulatory document:

Paragraph 42(2)(e) of the *Canada Business Corporations Act*
In accordance with paragraph (*f*) of CFAO 19-27/H . . .

• letters referring to lines of verse (rhyme schemes):

The Shakespearean sonnet has an *abab, cdcd, efef, gg*
rhyme scheme.

• letter symbols or words used in legends to illustrations, drawings, photographs, etc. or within the body of the text to identify parts of the item concerned. Such words as *top, bottom, left, right, above, below, left to right* and *clockwise from left* are frequently encountered in this context:

United States negotiator Nitze, *left*, greets his Soviet
counterpart, Yuli Kvitsinsky, in Geneva.

6.11 Letters and terms in the sciences

Italicize the scientific (Latin) names of genera and species in botanical, zoological and paleontological matter:

The sugar maple (*Acer saccharum*) is a member of the family
Aceraceae.

Do not italicize the names of the larger subdivisions (phyla, classes, orders, families and tribes):

The order Primates includes modern man (*Homo sapiens*).

Italicize letters designating unknown quantities and constants, lines, etc. in algebraic, geometric and similar matter:

Let *n* be the number of molecules . . .
$5x \times a^2 - 2ab$

Note in the second example that no space is left between the numerical coefficients and the variables, and that the italics help to differentiate between the variable x and the multiplication sign. Correct spacing and italic type also help to distinguish between algebraic variables and SI symbols:

10x m

6a cm

10b L

Italicize quantity symbols such as l for length, m for mass and v for velocity in order to distinguish them from unit symbols such as "L" for litre, "m" for metre and "V" for volt, which are normally printed in roman type:

60 N $= m \times$ 12 m/s²

$m = 5$ kg

(N $=$ newton, $m =$ mass, and m $=$ metre)

Certain Latin prefixes and Greek and Roman letters used as prefixes to the names of chemical and biochemical compounds are italicized:

cis-dimethylethylene

β-lactose

N-acylneuraminic acid

M-xylene

A number of Greek and Roman letters used in statistical formulas and notations are italicized, among them:

P	probability of
μ	population mean
σ	population standard deviation
σ^2	population variance

6.12   Headings

Headings or subheadings of a document may be italicized in order to clarify its arrangement for the reader. See Chapter 11.12 for further information on this point.

Seven

Punctuation

7

Punctuation

7.01 Introduction

Punctuation serves primarily to help show the grammatical relationships between words, but it is also used to indicate intonation. Its role is to clarify, and this principle takes precedence over all precepts governing the use of individual marks of punctuation. In the interest of clarity, punctuation should be as consistent as possible within a given text. For clarity, too, some grammarians recommend the use of "close" punctuation: the insertion of punctuation marks wherever their omission might mislead the reader. Most readers, however, will be grateful to the writer who opts for a more "open" style, omitting punctuation when this can be done without creating ambiguity. Finally, punctuation should not be a chore; if a passage appears difficult to punctuate, it is probably in need of rephrasing.

The Period

7.02 Main purpose

The period marks the end of an affirmative sentence or sentence fragment:

> The executive assistant was hired on the strength of his curriculum vitae. No interview or examination. Just an analysis of his file.

The period is a "full stop." It stops the reader more fully than the colon, semicolon, comma or dash. Each of these marks of punctuation may, in many circumstances, be used in place of one of the others in order to lessen or intensify a break in the flow of the sentence or passage. In the following examples the period has replaced a weaker mark of punctuation in order to slow the reader down and focus his or her attention:

> The wheels of government grind exceeding slow. And with
> good reason.
> I don't know if you know the mental effect of a bromoseltzer.
> But it's a hard thing to commit suicide on.
> You can't.
> You feel so buoyant.
>
> —Stephen Leacock

In the following examples, the period has itself been replaced by a weaker mark of punctuation in order to bring the elements into a closer relationship:

> He never drew the wrong conclusions—he never drew any conclusions at all.

> The parliamentary process is either exciting or efficient; efficient is better.

7.03 Imperatives, exclamations and indirect questions

Use a period after a mild imperative or exclamation:

> Dear God, you gave me a voice, I didn't ask for it. So help me.
>
> —Louis Quilico

> We are sold for the price of a sheepskin.
>
> —Joseph Howe

A sentence that is interrogative in form may be imperative in function and thus take a period (see 7.09):

> Will you come this way, please.

Indirect questions are affirmative sentences and take a period, not a question mark (but see 7.09):

> It is important for managers to ask why annual performance objectives have not been met.

7.04 Ellipsis points

Use ellipsis points *(. . .)* to indicate a silence in dialogue, hesitation or interruption in a speech, a pause in the narrative or the passage of time. Used in this way, they are sometimes referred to as suspension points (or periods):

> —What is your approach to self-actualization?
>
> — . . .
>
> —Let me rephrase that.

> The Minister's speech dragged on and on . . . until, finally, the TV announcer's voice broke the monotony.

Ellipsis points may be substituted for *etc.* and similar expressions at the end of a list:

> nuts
> bolts
> screws
> . . .

Do not use ellipsis points to imply hidden meanings or to separate groups of words for emphasis, as is often done in advertising.

For the use of ellipsis points to indicate omissions in quotations, see 8.09.

7.05　Leaders

A row of dots (or short dashes), called leaders, is used in indexes and tables, including tables of contents, to help the reader align material separated by a wide space:

1. Period 1
2. Leaders 11

A series of dots is sometimes used in place of underlining to indicate where information (or a signature) is to be entered on a form:

Suggestion No. . . . .
Approved by . . . .

7.06　Other uses

Periods may replace parentheses after numerals or letters used to introduce items in a vertical list:

1. Logic
2. Grammar
   a. relative clause
   b. subordinate clause

A run-in sidehead should be followed by a period:

Punctuation. Punctuation is the art of. . . .

No period should be used at the end of any other form of heading, legend or the like, or after a date line or signature.

See 1.02 for the use of periods with abbreviations.

Short signboard messages do not require a final period:

No Trespassing　　　　　Employees Only

7.07　Spacing

A period at the end of a sentence or run-in heading is followed by a single space, as are periods used as ellipsis points; periods within abbreviations are not followed by any space.

The Question Mark

7.08　Main purpose

A question mark is placed at the end of a direct question, sometimes even if the sentence is declarative or imperative in form:

Doctor Livingstone, I presume?

Surely not?

Give him more time? Don't make me laugh.

I don't suppose you'd have another one in the same

colour?

7.09   Requests, indirect questions and other uses

Opinions differ as to whether a polite request of the type *May I . . .* , *Would you . . .* or *Will you . . .* requires the question mark. However, a question mark will look out of place after longer requests of this kind, especially if the sentence embodies straightforward affirmative elements:

> May I escort you to your car?

> Will you come this way, please.

> Will you please go—before I have you thrown out.

Although the question mark is normally omitted after indirect questions, one may be added if the sentence has the force of a request:

> I wonder if you could give me a dollar for the bus ride home?

Occasionally a question will incorporate an exclamatory element. The writer must then decide whether the interrogative or the exclamatory element is to be given greater prominence:

> What hath God wrought!

> How many times must I tell you?

A question mark in parentheses (italicized in square brackets in quoted material) is inserted after information about which the writer is uncertain:

> Mr. Schwartz, who speaks with a German (?) accent, applied for the position last week.

A question mark inserted by way of ironic commentary, however, is likely to create an unprofessional impression and is best omitted.

Indicate missing digits with a question mark:

> Henri Potvin (1615—165?)

See Chapter 8 for the use of the question mark with quotation marks and other punctuation.

7.10   Spacing

A question mark is followed by one space.

The Exclamation Mark

7.11   Main purpose

The exclamation mark is an intensifier. It is used to indicate surprise, urgency, finality and the like. It is most often found after interjections, but also after ellipses, contractions and inversions and after certain onomatopoeic words:

Crash! went the filing cabinet.

but

The crash of the filing cabinet was heard far down the hall.

Sometimes the exclamation mark is used to convey a special intonation which the reader would not give the words if they were punctuated normally:

And I thought he was joking!

The exclamation mark is also used after forceful requests, wishes, invocations and commands:

Would that I could!

Follow my white plume!

—Sir Wilfrid Laurier

7.12   Miscellaneous

An exclamation mark, usually in parentheses (italicized in square brackets in quoted material), is sometimes used to indicate incredulity on the part of the writer. As with the analogous use of the question mark, this is a technique easily overdone:

Mr. Jones asserted that never in his long and distinguished (!) political career had he taken a bribe.

When exclamations occur in a series they are usually separated by commas:

Several honourable members: "Hear, hear!"

However, two interjections may be combined with no intervening punctuation:

Oh no!

Where the words themselves suffice to convey the emphasis, or where the sentence or clause is more properly a question, do not use an exclamation mark:

Another project failure like this, and we are finished.

Who knows? Who cares?

Exclamations are of necessity short. An exclamation mark should never appear at the end of a long sentence unless it is intended to intensify only the last word or words.

The exclamation mark should be used as sparingly as possible. Emphatic wording is usually more effective than emphatic punctuation.

7.13 Spacing

An exclamation mark is followed by one space.

The Comma

7.14 General

The comma is the most frequently misused punctuation mark, and many of the rules governing its use are vague and riddled with exceptions. The writer must frequently rely on his or her own judgment and should be guided by considerations of clarity more than by any particular set of rules. Most modern grammarians would add, "If in doubt, leave it out." Yet the comma is also the mark most often incorrectly omitted.

7.15 Restrictive/non-restrictive

Most difficulties with the use of the comma hinge on the distinction between restrictive and non-restrictive sentence elements. A restrictive word, phrase or clause adds to the words it modifies a "restrictive" or defining element which is essential to the meaning of the whole, and should therefore not be separated by a comma or other mark of punctuation. A non-restrictive element provides incidental or supplementary information which does not affect the essential meaning; it should be set off by a comma or commas.

Compare

> The senators who had objected most strongly to the shift in policy were quick to acknowledge the error in their thinking.   (restrictive)

and

> The senators, who had objected most strongly to the shift in policy, were quick to acknowledge the error in their thinking.   (non-restrictive)

a) There are exceptions to the general rule for punctuating restrictive and non-restrictive elements. An introductory phrase or clause, especially if it is a long one, is often followed by a comma whether it is restrictive or not:

> Of all election issues, the place of minorities in society is the most sensitive.

> When choosing between two approaches, it is important to consult experts in the field.

> **but**

> In the course of the conference some provincial leaders reversed their position on native rights.

Each of the above sentences could have been correctly punctuated either with or without the comma. But if an introductory subordinate clause is followed by a conjunctival *now*, *then* or *still*, the comma should be retained in order to avoid having these words read as adverbs of time. In the following example

> When there are enough good Moslems in a society, that society will inevitably become an Islamic society. If that Islamic society establishes itself and endures then, no less inevitably, it will produce an Islamic state.

the word *then* appears to be an adverb of time belonging to the *if* clause, but it in fact introduces the main clause and should be preceded by a comma.

The introductory phrase may consist of an adjective or participle separated from its noun by the definite or indefinite article:

> Unprepared, the team was no match for its opponents.

> Clearly upset by the heckling, the speaker stopped for a moment to regain his composure.

Conversely, it is sometimes possible to omit the commas which ordinarily set off non-restrictive elements, without obscuring the meaning. This is especially true of short adverbial expressions:

> Her words were of course unheeded.
> All the same he had no compunction about slipping the waiter a few dollars to be on the safe side.

In such sentences the addition of commas not strictly needed for clarity gives emphasis to the elements thus enclosed:

> Her words were, of course, unheeded.

b) One form of non-restrictive expression is the **absolute** construction: a phrase bearing no grammatical relationship to any word or group of words in the remainder of the sentence. Such phrases are followed by a comma:

> To tell the truth, I wish this chapter were finished.

> The chapter completed, I returned to my former duties.

Note the following errors in the punctuation of absolute expressions:

> The investigation had been completed, and the results, having been known for some time, the public was anxiously waiting for heads to roll.
>   (*no comma after* results)

> We were unable to answer her questions. The truth being that we hadn't given the matter much thought.
>   (*comma or dash after* questions)

c) Parenthetic expressions are non-restrictive and therefore require commas:

> We could see that, if not actually rejected out of hand, the plan was far from popular with senior management.

If a parenthetic expression is removed from the sentence, the remainder of the sentence should read as a coherent, grammatically correct whole. For example, the sentence

> The task force wanted to show that it was as good, if not better, than its predecessors.

is unacceptable because "as good ... than" is incorrect English. The sentence should be recast thus:

> ... it was as good as, if not better than, its predecessors.

Occasionally it may be expedient to omit the first of the pair of commas around a parenthetic expression:

> But without realizing it, he had sparked a whole new controversy.

The parenthetic phrase here is "without realizing it."

Both commas can sometimes be safely omitted:

> But without realizing it he had sparked a whole new controversy.

Under no circumstances, however, should the second comma be omitted while the first is retained:

> But, without realizing it he had sparked a whole new controversy.

Parenthetic expressions may be set off by parentheses or dashes instead of commas, depending on the degree of emphasis or pause desired, or the length of the expression. Compare:

> Jane (evidently) had no stake in seeing the dispute continue.

> Jane evidently had no stake in seeing the dispute continue.

> Jane, evidently, had no stake in seeing the dispute continue.

> Jane—evidently—had no stake in seeing the dispute continue.

A common error occurs with parenthetic phrases following the conjunction *that*. The comma that belongs after the conjunction is often placed before it instead:

> The odd thing was, that no matter how he tried, he couldn't think where he had left the document.

d) Restrictive and non-restrictive appositives should be carefully distinguished. The latter are set off by commas, while the former are not:

St. John of the Cross
Graham St. John, of Hoary Cross

Her painting *Reflections* drew a poor response from the public.
Her first painting, *Etude,* has been little studied.

As in the case of parenthetic expressions, the comma following a non-restrictive appositive cannot be omitted:

The statement by the Secretary of State for External Affairs, Mr. Clark last week that chances of an agreement with Moscow are minimal was soundly based.
   (*comma missing after* Clark)

Non-restrictive appositives in final position are usually preceded by a comma:

Our supreme governors, the people.

Often, however, the comma is replaced by a colon or dash:

Realism: a quality that no successful businessman can do without.

John Diefenbaker—perhaps the greatest man who ever came out of Saskatchewan.

If the appositive contains internal commas, it is best introduced by a mark other than a comma. In the following example, a colon would have been an improvement over the comma after *dignitaries*:

The Pope was greeted by a number of dignitaries, Mr. and Mrs. Mulroney, the Governor General, the Archbishop of Ottawa, etc.

e) The annunciatory expressions *namely, that is* and *for example* should usually be followed by a comma. They may be preceded by a comma, a dash or a period, or the matter which the expression introduces may be enclosed in parentheses, depending on the emphasis desired.

Plans for Senate reform should be honestly and objectively assessed, that is, bearing in mind only the public good.

The abbreviations *i.e.* and *e.g.* need not be followed by a comma.

Note that the expression *such as* is used to introduce an example, not an appositive, and therefore is not followed by a comma. It may be preceded by a comma or other punctuation, as required in the sentence.

f)   Vocative forms are non-restrictive and are set off by commas:

> Gentlemen, where I come from, a black-hearted bastard
> is a term of endearment.
> —Donald Gordon

> Awake, my country, the hour is great with change!
> —Charles Roberts

Similarly, exclamations and interjections are set off by commas (or exclamation marks):

> God, what a lot we hear about unhappy marriages, and
> how little we hear about unhappy sons and daughters.
> —Robertson Davies

7.16   Co-ordinate elements

Elements of equal rank or relation in a sentence are said to be co-ordinate. The co-ordinate elements may be words or phrases in a series, or they may be entire clauses.

a)   Items in a series may be separated by commas:

> Complacency, urbanity, sentimentality, whimsicality

They may also be linked by co-ordinating conjunctions such as *and* or *or*:

> economists, sociologists and political scientists
> the good, the bad and the ugly

Opinions differ on whether and when a comma should be inserted before the final *and* or *or* in a sequence. In keeping with the general trend toward less punctuation, the final comma is best omitted where clarity permits, unless there is a need to emphasize the last element in the series. This comma is usually omitted in the names of firms and always before an ampersand:

> Deeble, Froom & Associates Ltd.

> Cohen, Hansen and Larose

On the other hand, it is usually inserted if the items in the series are phrases or clauses of some length, or if omission of the comma might lead to ambiguity or misunderstanding:

> Tenders were submitted by Domicile Developments Inc.,
> East End Construction, Krista, and Ryan and Scheper.

A comma is also required before *etc.*:

> He brought in the wine, the glasses, etc.

A more complex situation occurs when apposition commas are used together with co-ordinating commas, as illustrated below:

> Carla Tavares, a recent MBA graduate and three students

Here the problem is compounded by the omission of the second apposition comma, after *graduate*. Such sentences should be rephrased so that no non-restrictive appositive occurs within a co-ordinate element:

> a recent MBA graduate named Carla Tavares, and three students

Alternatively, semicolons may be used to separate elements in a complex series (see also 7.25):

> Michael Cassidy, MP for Ottawa Centre; Peter Elzinga, MP for Pembina; Sheila Copps, MP for Hamilton East . . .

b) A comma is normally used to separate two main clauses in a compound sentence when they are joined by a co-ordinating conjunction (*and, but, or, nor, yet* or *for*):

> They are often called individualists, and in economic matters they were, but in social matters, the dominating concept was that of good neighbourliness. . . .
> —M. M. Fahrni

If the clauses are short or closely related, the commas may be omitted before *and, but, or* or *nor*:

> He opened the letter and then he read the contents.

> Life is short but art is long.

Co-ordinate clauses *not* joined by a co-ordinating conjunction are usually separated by a heavier mark of punctuation than the comma:

> When the white man came we had the land and they had the Bibles; now they have the land and we have the Bibles.
> —Chief Dan George

A comma will suffice, however, if the clauses are short, or if the writer wishes to lead the reader on to the following clause as quickly as possible:

> There are good regulations, there are bad regulations.

> It isn't the duration of the pilot project that bothers me, it's the size of the project team.

When a number of independent co-ordinate clauses follow one another, a comma should be used between each one except (usually) the last, in accordance with the rule for items in a series (see above):

> She investigated the matter, wrote a report, presented it to the committee and answered everyone's questions satisfactorily.

It is a common error to confuse a simple sentence having a compound predicate with a compound sentence requiring a comma between clauses. Note the difference between the following examples:

> She investigated the matter and then wrote a detailed report.

> She investigated the matter, and then the committee began its work.

Where the clauses of a compound sentence are joined by a conjunctive adverb (such as *however, instead, meanwhile, otherwise, similarly, so, still, then, therefore* or *yet*), a semicolon is usually called for, though a comma will often suffice before *so, then* and *yet*:

> Much of English-speaking Canada has been populated ... by a highly literate people, drawn in part from the educated classes of the Old Country, yet in its two hundred years of existence it has produced few books and not a single great one.
>> —E. A. McCourt

c) A series of adjectives modifying a noun may or may not be co-ordinate. The adjectives are co-ordinate if their order does not affect the meaning, in which case they should be separated by a comma. If they are not co-ordinate, that is, if one adjective modifies the phrase formed by the following adjective(s) plus the noun, then they should not be separated by a comma:

> a rich, creamy sauce

> **but**

> a naive domestic burgundy

Adjectives of both types may of course occur together:

> a tender, succulent young chicken

The rule stated above is, however, not an infallible guide. When in doubt omit the comma, as in:

> The plain honest truth is that he is a liar.

The final adjective in the series should not be separated from the following noun by a comma:

> Nations require strong, fair, open, decisive government.

d) Antithetic expressions are usually separated by a comma:

> This proposal is not to be tossed lightly aside, but to be hurled with great force.

However, short expressions of this type may not require a comma:

> The more wit the less courage.

7.17 Clarity and emphasis

Sometimes the reader will be led astray by a word or phrase which appears at first to be used in one sense but turns out from the context to be used in another. In all the following examples, commas should have been used in order to prevent misreading:

> In all his efforts were quite laudable. (In all, . . .)
>
> He was taken to the cleaners and left without any money, he soon grew desperate. (. . . and, left . . .)
>
> In the presence of Sir Henry James began to quiver.
> (. . . Sir Henry, James . . .)
>
> I was high up and far below I saw the globe of the earth.
> (. . . up, and . . .)

The comma can be a useful device for securing a pause or emphasis:

> I'm sure she'll be here, eventually.
>
> He had, once again, put himself in a no-win situation.
>
> The end had come, but it was not yet in sight.
> —John K. Galbraith

7.18 Omitted words

A comma may be used to indicate that words have been omitted:

> The African countries sent six representatives; the Asian countries, five.

Again, the comma may be omitted if clarity is not compromised.

See also 7.24.

7.19 Quotations, etc.

Place a comma after words introducing short direct quotations, declarations and direct questions (a colon is needed to introduce longer sentences):

> A politician once remarked, "Life is short; live it up."
>
> I repeat, No milk today.
>
> Ask yourself, Can I afford this?

Note the capital letter and the absence of quotation marks in the last two examples.

If the quotation or question follows a form of the verb *to be*, is in apposition to a noun, or is worked naturally into the syntax of the sentence, no comma is needed:

> What he actually said was "Play it, Sam."

> Did I give a satisfactory answer to the chairperson's question "Why are there so few women in management?"

> She asked us to "rephrase the question to make it less offensive."

It is also acceptable to omit the comma before quotations introduced by verbs of saying:

> He said "Have a nice day," fired a few shots, and ran.

7.20 Names and titles

Commas are used around titles and degrees within the body of a sentence:

> Charles Peabody, MD, PhD, was the first to arrive.

> Judith Foster, Chairperson of the External Affairs Committee, made the opening statement.

A comma is placed between a surname and a given name or initials if the surname is written first:

> Mammouri, Muhammad
> Fortin, M. A.

Chinese and Vietnamese names are an exception. They are written with the family name first and no comma:

> Mao Zedong
> Ho Chi Minh

7.21 Dates, geographical names and addresses

Use a comma to separate the day of the week from the date and the place from the date:

> Friday, February 13   but Friday the thirteenth
> Hull, February 13

If the date is written in the order day-month-year, no commas are required before, after or between the components of the date:

> The meeting of 1 January 1985 did little to allay tensions.

If, however, the order given is month-day-year, the day and year are separated by a comma, and the year should normally be followed by a comma within the body of a sentence or sentence equivalent:

> January 1, 1985, marked the beginning of a new era.

> On April 16, 1985, certain additional provisions of the Charter of Rights took effect.

Similarly, a comma separates a place name from the name of a province or the abbreviation for that province, and the province's name or abbreviation is normally followed by a comma within the body of a sentence or sentence equivalent:

> Swift Current, Saskatchewan, has applied to host the event.

> We arrived at Corner Brook, Nfld., the following day.

Use commas to separate address components, as illustrated:

> 340 Laurier Ave. West, Ottawa, Ontario K1A 0P8, is our mailing address.

Note that the postal code is followed, but not preceded, by a comma when the address forms part of a sentence.

7.22 Commas properly omitted

Do not use commas between the name and the number of an organizational unit:

> Teamsters Union Local 91
> Loyal Order of Moose 1765

Omit commas in numerical expressions such as the following:

> 2 years 6 months 7 days
> a 2-year 6-month sentence
> a 3-minute 50-second mile
> 1 h 12 min 55 s

Note that, as a general rule, commas interrupt the flow of a sentence and should therefore not be used where they do not contribute to clarity. A sentence requiring a large number of commas for clarity is probably a poorly constructed sentence in need of rephrasing.

7.23 Spacing

The comma is followed by a single space.

The Semicolon

7.24 Between independent clauses

The semicolon is used between independent clauses not joined by a co-ordinating conjunction but too closely related to be separated by a period:

> Inflation makes misery unanimous; it is universal poverty.
> —Arthur Meighan

> In theory the Commons can do anything; in practice, it can do little.
> —John Turner

If the clauses are short and parallel, a comma may replace the semicolon:

> **I'll talk, you listen.**

Clauses joined by a co-ordinating conjunction may also be separated by a semicolon (instead of a comma) if they are the last two of a series of clauses separated by semicolons:

> **It is easy to jump on the bandwagon; it is easy to wash one's hands of an issue; but it is not easy to take a position contrary to that of the majority and to defend it at all costs, to the bitter end.**

Use a semicolon if a sharper break is required than could be achieved with a comma (for emphasis or to convey antithesis):

> **The politician proclaims that we live in the best of all possible worlds; and the unemployed worker fears this is true.**

Clauses joined by a conjunctive adverb usually require a semicolon between them, though a comma may suffice if the clauses are short:

> **He loved his country; therefore he fought and died for it.**

> **I think, therefore I am.**

Elliptical clauses are conventionally separated from each other and from the introductory clause by semicolons, with commas often marking the ellipses (see 7.18):

> **To err is human; to forgive, divine.**

The semicolon can be replaced by a comma, however, provided that the comma marking the ellipses can be dropped:

> **One best seller makes a successful writer, ten a great one.**

7.25 Co-ordinate elements

Semicolons may be used in place of commas to separate parallel elements in a series if these elements are complex or contain internal punctuation, or if greater emphasis is desired:

> **Genesis 2:3; 4:15,17; 5:9−14**

> **Nature is often hidden; sometimes overcome; seldom extinguished.**

Even a series of parallel subordinate clauses may be separated in this manner, provided that the resulting punctuation is not apt to confuse the reader.

7.26 Misuse and overuse

Although most writers tend to underuse rather than overuse the semicolon, a writing style which employs a large number of semicolons is likely to be heavy and dull. Consider using the dash, colon or comma instead.

7.27 Spacing

The semicolon is followed by a single space.

The Colon

7.28 Between independent clauses

The colon may be used between two independent clauses not joined by a conjunction if the second clause explains, illustrates or enlarges upon the first. In such sentences a semicolon would also be correct, but less effective:

> An understanding of the connection between oral and written punctuation can be of great help to the student: it will enable him to punctuate his written sentences more accurately and more confidently.
> —*Effective English for Business*

> We are now at the point when an awakening bitterness follows a night of intoxication: an ebb of retribution now follows in the wake of a flood-tide of railway construction.
> —Arthur Meighan

A colon may be used between two clauses in antithesis:

> Man proposes: God disposes.

The work of the colon could have been done by a period or even a comma in the above example.

7.29 Annunciatory function

Today the colon is used primarily to introduce the words that follow it. It introduces a list, a formal quotation or a formal statement:

> There are three kinds of lies: lies, damned lies, and statistics.

> The first sentence of the circular was unequivocal: "The purpose of this circular is to announce the termination of the policy respecting federally administered prices."

> Simply put, the directive says this: Employees may smoke in their own offices, but nowhere else.

Short quotations or declarations, however, are usually introduced by a comma (see 7.19).

7.30 Miscellaneous

The colon is sometimes used between words that rhyme or are otherwise related or compared. No space is left before or after the colon:

> room:doom   black:white

In business letters and printed speeches, a colon follows the salutation:

> Dear Mr. Fox:

In personal letters, the colon is usually replaced by a comma:

Dear Susan,

The colon is used to separate titles from subtitles. It is followed by a single space:

Canada: A Story of Challenge

In references to books, plays, etc., colons separate chapter and verse, volume and page and act and scene, with no space on either side of the colon:

Numbers 7:11

History of Upper Canada, II:791

Fortune and Men's Eyes, I:i

Location and name of publisher are also separated by a colon. The colon is followed by a single space:

Ottawa: University of Ottawa Press

See Chapter 9 for further information on the use of the colon in reference matter.

See Chapter 5 for uses of the colon with numerical expressions.

7.31 Misuse

A colon should never be placed at the end of a title or heading standing on a separate line from the text it introduces; nor should a colon ever be followed by a dash *(:—)*.

7.32 Spacing

The colon is followed by one space, except as noted in 7.30.

Parentheses

7.33 General

Parentheses, or round brackets, are used to enclose additional information serving to explain, amplify or provide comments on adjacent material. Commas and dashes are also used for this purpose (see 7.15(d), 7.46 and 7.48). Parentheses, however, are generally used for words that are less closely related to the rest of the sentence than material which would be set off by dashes or commas. They are also more convenient for parenthetic elements which run to some length or contain internal punctuation, although it is best to avoid lengthy parentheses wherever possible.

7.34   Clarification

Parentheses may save the writer from other punctuation problems, such as the confusion created when apposition commas and enumeration commas appear together, as illustrated below:

> Carla Tavares (a recent MBA graduate) and three students

> **not**

> Carla Tavares, a recent MBA graduate, and three students

7.35   Punctuation with parentheses

A parenthesis consisting of a complete sentence does not take an initial capital and final period unless it stands alone between two complete sentences:

> To achieve the best possible results, adopt a combination of the CPM and PERT methods. (C. Jones presents a model of such a combination in the attached paper.) This will provide you with an effective, low-cost control mechanism.

An opening parenthesis should not be preceded by any other mark of punctuation unless the parentheses are being used to enclose numbers or letters of enumeration (see 7.39):

> I am (I hope) reliably informed that there is a spider ladder on sale.

After the closing parenthesis, any punctuation which would be appropriate in the absence of the parenthesis should still be used:

> I am (I hope), always have been and always will be an honest judge.

Before a closing parenthesis only a period, question mark, exclamation mark or quotation mark is permitted.

7.36   Afterthoughts and asides

Parentheses de-emphasize the words they contain, which often take the form of an afterthought or aside:

> Hitler (no mean orator himself) was enthusiastic in his praise of Mr. Chamberlain's speech.

An important afterthought, however, should be preceded by a dash or other mark of punctuation:

> Finally the Computer Operations Branch agreed to follow through on the auditor's recommendations—which is what it should have done six months earlier if it had had the best interests of the organization at heart.

In transcripts, use parentheses to enclose information on one of the speakers:

> **The Hon. Benoît Bouchard (Secretary of State of Canada):**
> Mr. Speaker, I support this initiative.

Parentheses should not alter the flow of the sentence in which they are inserted; the rest of the sentence should make sense if the parenthetic element is removed. The following is incorrect:

> She had to forfeit her acting appointment (not to mention her bilingualism bonus) and she got no sympathy on either count.

7.37 Parentheses within parentheses

If you cannot avoid placing parenthetic material within other parenthetic material, use square brackets within the round brackets (see 7.41) or use a combination of parentheses and dashes:

> He worked hard—twelve hours a day (and no bonus for overtime), seven days a week—until the task was completed.

7.38 Legal documents

In legal texts, parentheses are used to enclose numerals previously written out:

> one thousand nine hundred and eighty-four (1984)

7.39 Letters and numerals

Individual letters or groups of letters may be enclosed within parentheses:

> Language(s) spoken in the home _____

Numerals or letters of enumeration may be followed by a closing parenthesis or by a period. When such numerals or letters appear within a paragraph, enclose them in parentheses:

> 4. Work plan
>   a) Evaluation
>   b) Training

> Guidelines for writers: (1) Be concise. (2) Write idiomatically. (3) Proofread carefully.

See 5.22 and 6.10 regarding references to sections of legislation. See Chapter 9 for the use of parentheses in reference matter.

Square Brackets

7.40 General

Square brackets, often simply called *brackets*, are more disconnective than parentheses. They are used to enclose material too extraneous for parentheses.

Since they do not appear on most typewriter keyboards, square brackets usually have to be inserted by hand. They can also be approximated by means of a combination of obliques and hyphens. Round brackets (parentheses) are commonly used in place of square brackets, but care should be taken to ensure that this does not mislead the reader. A slightly unprofessional typing job may sometimes be preferable to unprofessional punctuation.

Use brackets for editorial comments or additional information on material written by someone else. To use ordinary parentheses for this purpose would give the impression that the inserted words were those of the person quoted. See 8.04, 8.10, 8.14 and 9.24 for detailed information and examples.

7.41 Use within parentheses

When one set of parentheses is to be placed within another, replace the inner parentheses with square brackets (though dashes may be used instead—see 7.37). Parentheses within parentheses should be used sparingly, however, except in legal and scholarly texts:

> *Acadia* (from *Algatem* ["dwelling here and there"])

Square brackets may also be used in place of round brackets where two or more sets of the latter would otherwise occur in succession:

> in 3(a) [according to Bixby's enumeration] . . .
> Here, f(x) [cf. s. 8.3] reaches a maximum when . . .

Braces

7.42 Use

Braces are used to link two or more lines of writing:

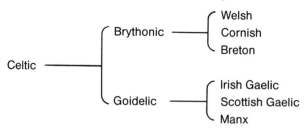

They are also used to group items in formulas and equations. See 7.43.

7.43 Multiples

In mathematical usage, the preferred order for multiple brackets is as follows:

$$\{[(\{[(\quad)]\})])]\}$$

Note that square brackets enclose round brackets, in contrast to the practice in non-mathematical usage.

The Em Dash

7.44 General

The em dash, often simply called a *dash*, is usually typed as two hyphens, with no space before or after. In most of its uses the em dash is simply a substitute for a colon, semicolon or comma, but it indicates a more emphatic or abrupt break in the sentence, or a less formal style.

7.45 Enumerations

Use a dash, not a colon, to enclose a list of terms that does not end the sentence:

> A number of processes—gassing, electroplating, soldering, casting, etc.—are used in the copper industry.

not

> A number of processes: gassing, electroplating, soldering, casting, etc., are used in the copper industry.

7.46 Interruptions, pauses, afterthoughts, clarifications and emphasis

Like parentheses, a dash may be used at the end of an unfinished or interrupted statement or a pause, as in transcripts:

> I have indicated that the appointment of the judge was terminated—or rather was not terminated but came to—
>
> **Some Hon. Members:** Oh, oh!

Here the dashes are used to indicate, first, a pause and clarification and, second, an interruption.

The dash may be used to introduce an afterthought, correction or repetition:

> Who will oppose—who are now opposed to the union?

It may similarly be used to set off an emphatic ending or one which contrasts with the remainder of the sentence:

> To write imaginatively a man should have—imagination.

Dashes give greater emphasis to parenthetic material than do commas or parentheses. If the parenthetic material contains internal punctuation or forms a complete sentence, the commas that might have been used to enclose it should be replaced by dashes or parentheses, depending on the degree of emphasis desired or the strength of the relationship to the rest of the sentence. Parentheses are generally used to enclose material more remote from the main thrust of the sentence, dashes for material more closely related:

> This country is something that must be chosen—it is so easy to leave—and if we do choose it we are still choosing a violent duality.
>
> —Margaret Atwood

7.47 Summarizing

A dash is sometimes inserted before the final portion of a sentence to clarify its relationship to the rest of the sentence, often with the help of a summarizing pronoun such as *all* or *these* or with the repetition of key words:

> Rich stores of minerals, good agricultural land, forests stretching over millions of acres, coastal waters teeming with fish, and energetic and enterprising people—all these assure Canada a bright future.

7.48 Material in apposition

Explanatory material in apposition may be set off by dashes to secure greater emphasis than would be achieved with a colon or commas or to avoid confusion with commas within the apposition:

> Patience—a minor form of suffering, of despair, disguised as a virtue.

7.49 Headings

A dash may be used to separate the heading of a chapter or the like from the description of its contents or to separate subheadings within a chapter or section, as in a catalogue:

> GELATIN MEMBRANE FILTERS, White, Plain, Sartorius—A water soluble filter developed solely for....

> Appendix A—Table of Symbols
> ISO 337-1973 Road vehicles—50 semi-trailer fifth wheel
> coupling pin—Dimensions

7.50 Lists and tables

It is sometimes used in place of enumeration numerals or letters in a drop list:

> 3. Service to the public
> —enquiries answered
> —brochures sent out
> —complaints investigated

It can represent *nil* or *unknown* in a list of figures:

	Atomic weight	Density	Melting point
Actinium	227	—	—
Aluminum	26.98	2.7	660

7.51 Punctuation with em dash

The dash may not be combined with any mark of punctuation other than quotation marks, the question mark, the exclamation mark and occasionally the period. In particular, the use of a colon-dash *(:—)* to introduce a quotation or a list has long since passed out of favour.

The En Dash

7.52 General

The en dash is longer than a hyphen and shorter than an em dash. It is typed as a hyphen but should not be confused with one. Where confusion is apt to result, the en dash should be replaced by an em dash (typed as two hyphens) rather than by a single hyphen.

7.53 Numerals

Its main use is to join inclusive numbers:

> pages 9–12
> 3–7° C **but** –3 to –7°C **not** –3 – –7° C
> Immanuel Kant (1724–1804)

7.54 Compound expressions

Use the en dash to join the names of two or more places:

> the riding of Kenora–Rainy River
> the Montreal–Windsor corridor

The Hyphen

7.55 Spelling and enunciation

Use the hyphen to spell out a word:

> s-p-e-l-l
> Where did you put the c-a-n-d-y?

Hyphens also indicate slow, deliberate enunciation:

> im-pos-si-ble
> Rai-aid!

See 2.10(b), 5.05 and 5.08 for the use of hyphens with numerical expressions.

The Oblique

7.56 General

The oblique, also known as a *solidus, slant (line), bar, virgule, diagonal, stroke* or *slash*, should never be used instead of a hyphen at the end of a line of ordinary prose to indicate word division.

Oblique strokes are sometimes used to replace square brackets on typewriters which lack these (see 7.40).

Between individual words, letters or symbols, the oblique is typed with no space on either side. Between longer groupings which contain internal spacing, the oblique should have a space on either side. When the oblique falls between clauses or longer phrases, it is usually typed with no space before and a single space after.

7.57 Abbreviations

The oblique is used in certain abbreviations:

c/o	care of	i/c	in charge
w/o	without	n/a	not applicable
a/c	account	A/Director	Acting Director

It can be used as a symbol for *per*:

km/h N/m^2

Do not use the oblique to represent *per* more than once in a single expression:

2.7 m·s^{-2} **not** 2.7 m/s/s

Nor should it be used with expressions of quantity written in full:

metres per second **not** metres/second

7.58 Numerals

The oblique is sometimes used in fractions, especially when set into a line of type, or when they would be ungainly in the form $\frac{a}{b}$:

She covered 2 1/3 lengths in 70 seconds.

Use it with ellipsis points and a numeral at the lower right-hand corner of a page to indicate that the text continues on the following page:

.../2

7.59 Alternatives and headings

An oblique may indicate alternatives:

He/She will perform the following duties.
Canada and/or the United States

A similar use is seen in bilingual titles such as *L'Actualité Terminologique / Terminology Update.*

Oblique strokes may separate headings on a form:

Division/Branch
Series/Cert. No.

The Apostrophe

7.60 Possession

The primary use of the apostrophe is to indicate possession.

A word which does not end in a sibilant (*s* or *z* sound) forms the possessive by the addition of *'s*:

a dog's breakfast   Toronto's CN Tower

Note that it is the pronunciation, not the spelling, which determines the possessive form. The word *conscience* ends in a sibilant; *Illinois* does not. Plural forms which do not end in a sibilant are no exception to the general rule:

women's   children's

Plurals ending in a sibilant take only the apostrophe:

the ministers' responsibilities
developing countries' needs

Regarding the appropriate form for singular words which end in a sibilant, pronunciation is again the determining factor. If it would be natural to pronounce an extra *s*, add *'s*; if an additional *s* would be difficult to pronounce, add only an apostrophe:

Joyce's *Ulysses*
Ulysses' wanderings
the boss's office

Since awkwardness of pronunciation is the basic criterion, the decision to add or omit a possessive *s* ultimately depends on the writer's own sensitivities. One option is to rephrase:

the strength of a lioness **rather than** a lioness'(s) strength
the ramblings of Joyce's Ulysses
rather than Joyce's Ulysses' ramblings

7.61 Compounds

Figurative compounds of the sort *bull's-eye* or *crow's-nest* retain *'s* in the plural:

bull's-eyes   crow's-nests

Bulls' eyes would be the eyes of bulls, *crows' nests* the nests of crows.

When the possessive of a compound noun or a noun phrase is formed, add *'s* to the last word only, unless there is a possessive relation between the words within the phrase itself:

> someone else's problem
>
> her brother-in-law's address
>
> John's father's problem
>
> the Attorney General's decision

7.62 Two nouns

If possession is shared by two or more subjects, add *'s* to the last word only:

> Adam and Eve's progeny
> Burton and Taylor's marriage
> Groucho, Chico and Harpo's antics

To indicate individual possession, *'s* is added to each element in the series:

> Abraham's and Lot's progeny
> Burton's and Taylor's marriages

7.63 Geographical names

The apostrophe is often omitted in geographical names:

> Gods Lake   Humphreys Mills
>
> **but**   **but**
>
> St. John's   Land's End

Note also *Saint John* (city in New Brunswick) and *Hudson Bay*—but *Hudson's Bay Co.* Check the *Gazetteer of Canada* or some other reliable reference work when in doubt.

7.64 Institutions and organizations

The *'s* is often omitted in names of institutions, especially in the case of plural nouns which are adjectival rather than strictly possessive:

> teachers college **but** inmates' committee
> veterans hospital **but** officers' mess

The official or customary form should be used, whatever it may be.

7.65 Its

Note that there is no apostrophe in the possessive forms *yours, hers* and *its*. *It's* is always a contraction of *it is*.

7.66   Contractions

Apostrophes represent omitted letters in contractions or omitted figures in dates:

> It's the best of its kind.   the class of '67
> Treasury Board didn't agree.   the crash of '29

If two or more omissions occur within a word, only the last is normally indicated. If letters are omitted from both the beginning and the end of a single word or a compound, only the first omission is usually indicated:

> shan't   ain't
> flu   **or**   'flu
>
> **but**
>
> fo'c'sle   'tain't

7.67   Plurals

Certain plurals are sometimes written with 's. These include:
- abbreviations whose appearance would otherwise be ambiguous or confusing (see 1.03) and the plurals of lower-case letters, symbols and numerals:

> x's
> a's and w's
> +'s and −'s
> 6's

Another solution is to italicize the letter, symbol or numeral in question (see 6.08 and 6.11).

- cited words:

> no if's, and's or but's
>
> **but**
>
> the **ANDs** and **ORs** in a computer program

- words not conveniently pluralized:

> all the Toms, Dicks, Harrys and Louis's
> all the Lao's in Laos

Eight

Quotations and quotation marks

8

Quotations
and
quotation marks

8.01 Introduction

The main use of quotation marks is to set off the exact words of a speaker or written source from the main body of a text. The quotation may consist of one or more complete sentences or paragraphs, parts of a sentence or paragraph or as little as one word. As an alternative to the use of quotation marks (**run-in** format), direct quotations may be indicated by means of indention and/or reduced leading (space between lines) or type size (**set-off** or **block** format). Whichever format is adopted, the quoted matter should normally be faithfully reproduced in every detail: the spelling, punctuation and other characteristics of the original may not be changed without good reason.

Bear in mind, too, that excessive use of quotations can mar the appearance of a page and make it difficult for the reader to follow the ideas being presented; it is often better to paraphrase, use indirect speech or give a summary of the ideas concerned in your own words—in each instance accompanied by a footnote providing the source of the information. Quotations are justified if the intention is to demonstrate or typify a particular characteristic, style or wording, or to compare quotations; if the material is striking, memorable or well-known; or if the quotation itself is an example or proof of what is being discussed, as in the case of legal evidence.

For information on capitalization in quotations, see 4.02(c); on the use of a comma or colon before quoted matter, see 7.19 and 7.29.

8.02 Run-in format

Use the run-in format when the quoted matter is not more than fifty words or five lines long:

The Minister said, "Prospects for growth are not good."

The quotation remains within the body of the paragraph.

Because the run-in format does not require indention, the writer enjoys some latitude in positioning the clause or phrase (the **annunciatory** element) that introduces the quotation.

Note that when a quotation is interrupted by other matter, the quotation marks are repeated before and after each part of the quotation:

> "In a narrower sense," the Minister added in her report, "governments are becoming increasingly worried about large spending deficits. The chances of still higher deficits, as tax revenues falter and spending pressures mount in a weak economy, are very great."

If you decide to insert the annunciatory clause between two items that were separate sentences in the original or have become separate sentences in the quotation, capitalize the first word of the second sentence, i.e. of the second part of the quotation:

> "In a narrower sense governments are becoming increasingly worried about large spending deficits," the Minister added in her report. "The chances of still higher deficits, as tax revenues falter and spending pressures mount in a weak economy, are very great."

Note also that the annunciatory clause ends with a period.

8.03 Punctuation and grammar in run-in quotations

Place commas and periods within closing quotation marks, whether or not they were included in the original material:

> **Original**
>
> The emergence of fifth-generation computers is a challenge for Canadian industry as a whole. Our prosperity depends on our keeping pace with the Japanese and Americans in this field over the coming decades.

> **Run-in quotation**
>
> "The emergence of fifth-generation computers is a challenge for Canadian industry as a whole," the Deputy Minister pointed out. "Our prosperity depends on our keeping pace with the Japanese and Americans in this field."

However, when a very high degree of accuracy is required (as in a legal context), it may be desirable to place any punctuation not part of the original document outside the quotation marks:

> This part of section 2 reads: "real and personal property of every description and deeds and instruments relating to or evidencing the title or right to property".

A closing dash, question mark or exclamation mark that was part of the quoted matter should be retained and placed inside the closing quotation marks if required to ensure the syntactical completeness and full meaning of the quotation. A closing semicolon or colon should normally be dropped and replaced with a period, comma or ellipsis points (see 8.09). Apart from periods and commas, punctuation introduced subsequently by the person quoting must be placed outside the closing quotation marks.

When a statement ends with a quotation that is itself a question or exclamation, no period is required after the closing quotation marks:

> One of the questions the Task Force on Canadian Unity asked was "What do Francophone minorities think is needed to ensure their survival and progress?"

> Commenting on the 1876 *Indian Act*, the Task Force on Canadian Unity notes that "an Indian could become enfranchised with the consent of his band and a certificate from a 'competent person' witnessing that he had demonstrated qualities sufficient to justify it!"

Similarly, if the quoted question or exclamation mark closes a sentence that is itself a question or exclamation, no additional punctuation is required outside the closing quotation marks:

> Was I wrong in minimizing the importance of the chairperson's question "Why are there so few women in science?"

Quotations that follow annunciatory clauses ending in *that* also require a grammatical change—from first person to third person pronouns, possessive adjectives and verbs:

Original

> I have great sympathy for the Francophones wanting to speak their own language and wanting to keep their own culture because I also want my own language and culture. My English culture includes the monarchy, and I resent it very much when anyone tries to abolish my culture or a part of it.
>
> —Statement to Task Force on Canadian Unity

Restructured version

> In his brief, a man from Vancouver claims to have great sympathy for the Francophones wanting to speak their own language and wanting to keep their own culture because he too wants his own language and culture. He points out that his English culture includes the monarchy and that he "[resents] it very much when anyone tries to abolish [his] culture or a part of it."

Note that if several changes of this kind would have to made within the same quotation, the material should be presented entirely in indirect speech.

8.04   Indirect speech

Material reproduced in indirect (reported) speech within the body of a paragraph does not have to be changed significantly. The first example in 8.02 may be restructured to read:

> The Minister said that prospects for growth were not good.

The verb in the subordinate clause shifts from the present tense of direct speech to the past tense in keeping with the rules of tense sequence. Likewise, a verb that was in the future tense in direct speech often takes the conditional form in indirect speech. Thus if the Minister's words had been "There will be no growth for some time," the indirect form would be:

The Minister said that there would be no growth for some time.

However, the present and future tenses may be retained if the actions or situations referred to are still current or future at the time of quotation:

The Minister said that there will be no growth this year.

Alternatively, a blend of direct and indirect speech may be preferred when a particular part of the original statement is to be highlighted:

The Minister said that prospects for growth were not good and that governments "[were] becoming increasingly worried about large spending deficits."

Because the first subordinate clause verb is in the past tense, the tense of the verb within the quotation must be altered. This time, because direct speech is being retained and the speaker did not actually use the past tense, the editorial change has to be indicated by means of brackets (see also 8.10).

8.05 Paragraphing: run-in format

If more than one paragraph from the same source is being quoted using the run-in format, and if the paragraphs follow one another in the original, quotation marks are placed at the beginning of each paragraph and at the end of the last. Similarly, material quoted from a letter should carry quotation marks before the first line (usually the salutation) and after the last line (usually the signature), as well as at the beginning of each new paragraph. However, block quotations would be more appropriate in such cases.

8.06 Set-off or block format

A block quotation set off from the text is not enclosed in quotation marks. However, it requires indention and, particularly in manuscripts, reduced—usually single—spacing. Smaller print size is an alternative to single spacing.

8.07 Paragraphing: block format

If the block quotation begins with a complete sentence—whether or not this was the first sentence of the paragraph in the source document—the first line may be indented further in order to match the format of subsequent paragraphs in the quotation. When a number of paragraphs are being quoted, extra leading is required after each one.

8.08 Quotations within quotations

Material that was already a quotation in the source document or speech should be enclosed in single quotation marks when run into the text and in double quotation marks within block quotations. The same rules of punctuation apply (see 8.03):

Run-in

In his report on the Conference on Native Rights, John Sheppard writes: "Provincial leaders gave varying degrees of commitment yesterday to expanding aboriginal rights, but even the most sympathetic of them warned the process will require 'a considerable amount of time.' "

Block

In his report on the Conference on Native Rights, John Sheppard writes:

> Provincial leaders gave varying degrees of commitment yesterday to expanding aboriginal rights, but even the most sympathetic of them warned the process will require "a considerable amount of time."

In the rare event that a further quotation within a quotation occurs, it is enclosed again in double quotation marks:

> He answered, "I was told, 'Keep the document marked "Secret" in a safe place.' "

8.09 Omissions

Omission of material from a quoted passage, whether run in or block, should be indicated by ellipsis points positioned on the line and separated one type space from each other and the preceding text, including any punctuation marks.

Three spaced dots show that material within a sentence in the source document has been omitted. Punctuation immediately preceding the omitted words should be dropped if it does not serve a purpose in the quotation:

Original sentence

Commitments for public housing, to be rented according to an approved rent-to-income scale, and financed by CMHC loans to the provinces, totalled $244.4 million in 1978.
—Canada Year Book 1980—81

Quoted sentence with omission

The 1980−81 *Canada Year Book* states: "Commitments for public housing . . . totalled $244.4 million in 1978."

Note that the comma after *housing* has been dropped.[1]

In addition, three dots can represent omission of the first sentence of a paragraph in a block quotation. They can also indicate an interrupted sentence or a deliberately incomplete sentence:

> **Mr. Fulton:** Oh, one minute. Perhaps we could expand a little bit, then, into the forestry job question for B.C. I am sure Mr. Reed is abundantly aware of the . . .
>
> **The Vice-Chairman:** The answer will have to be given in writing.
>
> The critic said, "I realize the play has its good qualities, but . . ."

To represent omission of the last part of a quoted sentence, use four dots—a period immediately following the preceding word with no intervening space, then three spaced dots:

Complete quotation

> Dr. Fischer stressed that young girls, in elementary school and before, should acquire a basic body of scientific knowledge and develop an attitude of exploration. Studies have found that independent children have less protective mothers than passive children and that they also have higher visual-spatial scores.
> —Science Council of Canada, *Who Turns the Wheel?*

Quotation with omissions

> Dr. Fischer stressed that young girls, in elementary school and before, should acquire a basic body of scientific knowledge. . . . Studies have found that independent children have less protective mothers than passive children. . . .

---

1. The example illustrates the care that must be taken in presenting partial quotations. The omitted qualifying phrase is non-restrictive, that is, it is not required for the rest of the sentence to be syntactically correct and to make perfect sense on its own. Had the commas not been placed around it in the original, the phrase would have been restrictive in that it would have defined a certain type of housing and could not have been dropped without altering the meaning of its antecedent, *housing*, and misrepresenting the facts in the quotation. See also 7.15.

Four dots can also indicate omission of the first part of the second or a subsequent sentence or of a whole sentence or more within the quotation:

Complete quotation

The Canadian committee system is much less effective than it could be because of the high rate of substitutions and turnover permitted. Much of the problem with the Canadian committee system is that membership turnover is so high that few committees ever develop the continuity, expertise, and mutual trust that make a committee effective. A change of attitudes and habits is required and we suggest a new parliamentary convention that committee membership be stable.
—Royal Commission on Financial Management and Accountability, *Final Report*

Quotation with omissions

The Canadian committee system is much less effective than it could be because of the high rate of substitutions and turnover permitted. . . . We suggest a new parliamentary convention that committee membership be stable.

The four dots represent omission of a whole sentence and the beginning of the next. Note that the first letter after the ellipsis may be capitalized, even though it does not begin a new sentence in the original. In legal writing, indicate any such change by enclosing the capitalized letter in brackets.

The other kind of omission indicated by four dots is that of a paragraph or more. The three spaced dots immediately follow the period at the end of the preceding paragraph. If the next paragraph in the quotation begins with a sentence that does not open a paragraph in the original, it should be preceded by three ellipsis points after the usual indention.

A complete line of dots from the left-hand margin to the right-hand margin signifies the omission of more than one paragraph or page in a quotation consisting of widely scattered elements of the source document. A complete line of dots is also used to indicate the omission of one or more lines of poetry.

8.10   Insertions, alterations and parentheses

While every quotation must be scrupulously exact, you may wish to provide the reader with information to clarify items in the quotation. For example, you may feel it advisable to indicate to whom the possessive adjective refers in the following:

The official insisted: "We foresee no change in their environmental policy in the near future."

The clarification would be made by means of brackets:

The official insisted: "We foresee no change in [U.S.] environmental policy in the near future."

All explanatory material added to the original must be enclosed in brackets. If you need to indicate an error in the original, such as a misspelling, insert the Latin word *sic*, italicized and enclosed in brackets, immediately after the word concerned. The addition of [*sic*] assures the reader of the accuracy of the quotation and of your competence as a writer.

When used in this way, [*sic*] should not be followed by a period or an exclamation mark. Implicit comments on peculiarities of form or content by means of an exclamation mark or question mark enclosed in parentheses should be avoided.

If you wish to draw attention to specific parts of a quotation, underline or italicize them. The reader must be informed in a footnote, or in parentheses or brackets immediately following the quotation, by means of a phrase such as *Italics mine*, *Underlining mine* or *My emphasis*, that the emphasis was not in the original.

8.11 References to words as words

Matter following terms such as *means*, *marked*, *specified*, *as*, *referred to as*, *the word* and *the phrase* should be enclosed in quotation marks since the reader's attention is being deliberately drawn to its form, to words as words:

> The Canadian International Development Agency will be
> referred to as "the Agency" in this agreement.
> The French word *dotation* means "staffing."
> The package was marked "Fragile."

In some cases italicization, boldface type and underlining are alternatives to quotation marks (see 6.08).

8.12 Slang and technical terms; words used in an ironic or special sense

Slang and colloquial terms are often peculiar to one region and should be enclosed in quotation marks if they are foreign to the normal vocabulary of the intended readers:

> The prairie fire was finally "gunnybagged" with the help of
> local farmers.

Vernacular terms used for rhetorical effect in information documents and administrative reports are treated in the same way.

However, the enclosure of supposed slang or colloquial words in quotation marks is often unnecessary. The writer should first ascertain whether the term is now part of the standard language. If it is, quotation marks are not required. If the item is still a slang term, it is then necessary to determine whether using it, rather than a synonym that is standard, is warranted—for rhetorical effect or in order to demonstrate a person's or group's speech or style, for example.

Technical terms may be enclosed in quotation marks in non-technical writing:

> The steel has to be "cold-rolled" before further processing.

This practice, too, is often unnecessary in an era when the educated lay reader has some knowledge of modern science and engineering. Depending on the target readership, technical terms may not need special treatment.

Quotation marks can also enclose words used ironically:

> Many "experts" were called in for consultation.

> The party whip called the five renegade MPs in for a "full and frank discussion" of the issue.

Here again it is often possible to avoid quotation marks by using the preceding text to prepare the reader for the irony.

Words used in a special sense or juxtaposed to terms with which they are not usually associated require quotation marks:

> The mayor was considered a "stuffed shirt."

> There is a high-technology spillover which makes human communication with machines easier and is helping to create "intelligent" robots.

8.13 Titles

In both manuscripts and printed documents, quotation marks should enclose the titles of the following when those titles are presented within the body of the text, in footnotes and in bibliographies: articles from newspapers, magazines and periodicals; chapters of books; conferences and symposiums; songs and short musical compositions; poems from collections; dissertations and theses; unpublished manuscripts; lectures and papers; and radio and television programs.

8.14 Translation of quotations

There are several alternatives available to writers wishing to incorporate material from French-language or foreign-language documents in their work.

The material can be quoted as it stands, without a translation, as long as the Roman alphabet is used, the intended reader has sufficient knowledge of the source language and the context is explicit enough for the quotation to be understood. Once the decision to give a translation has been made, it is preferable to quote from a translation that has already been published or gained credibility in some other way (in a thesis, for example) than to provide one of your own.

Translations of short quotations, chapter headings, terms or titles of articles can be provided in brackets immediately after the closing quotation marks, as in the examples below:

> Chapter v, "Die Benennung" ["Terms"], contains an extensive description of rules for the construction of German words and terms.

> Chapters vi and vii contain an elaborate classification of *Zeichen* [signs].

> Wüster states: "Ein Schriftsonderzeichen ist jedes Zeichen, das kein Schriftgrundzeichen ist." ["A special writing character is any symbol which is not a main writing character."]

> The reader should consult Choul's article "Approches de la traduction technique" ["Approaches to technical translation"] for further information.

For a long quotation, give a translation in a footnote on the same page.

Whether you are presenting both the original and the translated quotation, a quotation from a published translation, or just your own translation, do not forget to identify the translation in a footnote (particularly for a published translation) or immediately before or after the quotation, as illustrated below:

> Belorgey goes on to say:

>> [*Translation*]
>> The considerable growth in governments' powers has won general acceptance because it is seen as the best way of providing the services needed by the community.

> As Jean Paré points out in the March 1983 issue of *L'Actualité*:

>> Today's revolution, even if it is a quiet one, will be tomorrow's dictatorship.
>> [*Translation*]

In each case the source of the original quotation must be referred to in a footnote.

An alternative to a source-language or translated quotation is an English paraphrase of the passage concerned, presented within the body of the paragraph and introduced by a phrase or clause such as *According to X* or *X notes that*. This approach is appropriate if emphasis is to be placed solely on the ideas contained in the source material, not on any special characteristics that can be communicated only through direct quotation.

Whether the passage finally presented is a paraphrase, a quotation from a published translation, or your own translation, take great care to ensure that the content of the original has been rendered accurately. Even translations from prestigious publishing houses often contain serious translation errors.

8.15 Abuse of quotation marks

Quotation marks should not enclose titles at the beginning of papers or articles, or chapter headings, epigraphs, well-known literary expressions, the words *yes* or *no* (except in direct speech), proverbs or well-known sayings, matter following *so-called*, or mathematical or scientific symbols.

Nine

Reference matter

9

Reference matter

9.01 Introduction

This chapter contains guidelines for the organization and presentation of footnotes, endnotes, bibliographies and indexes.

Notes and bibliographies are the means used by authors of books and articles in all fields to document the source of any quotations or ideas that are not their own. Footnotes and endnotes may also contain a reference to information found elsewhere in the book or article or provide supplementary or background data that cannot easily be incorporated in the body of the text. Indexes, on the other hand, never contain information; they guide the reader to information in the text.

Footnotes and Endnotes

9.02 Reference number

Footnotes and endnotes are generally referenced by means of a superscript (raised) numeral immediately following the item in question. Except for the dash, any punctuation mark immediately following the last word of the numbered item must precede the numeral:

> As Jones points out in a recent article,[1] the ambassador's criticism of the countries involved [2]—Cuba, Nicaragua and the Soviet Union—upset a number of delegates.

9.03 Footnotes

If only a few notes are required on each page of an article or a chapter and the note material is succinct, use the footnote format:

> In the United States, in contrast, approximately 49% of psychologists name either teaching or research as their principal activity, compared with only 31% for service functions.[1] Table 15 shows the numbers and proportions of English- and French-speaking[2] Canadians and of American and other foreign respondents in each of the principal work functions. It is estimated that 13−14% of Canadian psychologists are French-speaking.[3]

1. 1966 National Register of Scientific and Technical Personnel.

2. French-speaking Canadians were identified by their request for or return of the French-language version of the questionnaire. Further identification and response rates were confirmed through follow-up telephone contacts with non-respondents (see Appendix 3).

3. But see discussion by Dr. Belanger on p. 127.

Note that the longest footnote is still relatively short, that the footnote numeral is followed by a period and a space, and that the first letter of the second and subsequent lines in each footnote is aligned with the footnote numeral. In a manuscript, separate the footnotes from the body of the text with a short line beginning at the left margin and, where more than one line is required, use single spacing. Note that footnote 2 does more than refer the reader to another work or page for further information: it gives information on how facts presented in the text were ascertained and confirmed. Such a note is called a **content note,** as opposed to a **reference note,** and is useful for conveying supplementary data.

The example above illustrates page-by-page footnote numbering—that is, the first reference number on each page is 1. This format requires careful checking if the draft is to be retyped or printed. It is possible that the typist's or printer's page will not contain the same number of lines as the original and that a footnote reference originally at the bottom of a page and numbered accordingly might appear at the top of the following page; the established numerical order for each page would then be lost and the reference number would be on a different page from the actual note. To avoid this problem, number your references from 1 upward throughout the article or chapter; the typist or printer then merely has to ensure that enough space is left in the lower half of the page for all the required footnotes to be included.

9.04   Endnotes

Where notes are numerous and lengthy and include extensive comments by the author, use the endnote format to facilitate typing and cross-referencing and enhance the appearance of the text.

The references are numbered consecutively throughout the article or chapter, as in the case of footnotes, but the notes follow the article or chapter in a reference list on a new page. An endnote page should have a heading, as in the following example:

Notes to Chapter 2

1. S.B. Ryerson, *The Founding of Canada* (Toronto: Progress Books, 1963), p. 58—59.

2. Ryerson, p. 76.

3. *Encyclopedia Canadiana* (Ottawa: The Canadiana Company Limited, 1957), Vol. 4, p. 156.

4. S. Fraser, *The Letters and Journals of Simon Fraser, 1806—1808* (Toronto: Macmillan Company of Canada Limited, 1960), p. 231.

Whether footnotes or endnotes are used, number your references on a chapter-by-chapter basis in books in order to avoid the possibility of triple-digit references, which would result in excessive space between words.

9.05   Illustrative material and symbols

Footnotes to tables, charts and other illustrative material are not numbered with the text footnotes. Lower-case letters, a separate set of numbers, or special symbols (*, +, #, etc.) are required for each illustration, and the notes should be placed directly below it, not at the foot of the page or at the end of the article or chapter concerned.

Where two distinct series of footnotes are required (an author's notes on the one hand and a translator's or editor's notes on the other, or citation notes as opposed to substantive notes), asterisks may be used for the translator's, editor's or substantive notes. Translator's and editor's notes should in addition be clearly labelled as such.

In statistical tables, where asterisks can have an entirely different meaning, it is better to use raised letters for footnotes instead. Letters are in fact preferred in all tables consisting primarily of figures:

	1978	1984	1990[a]
Haiti	35	19	2
Canada[b]	1080	920	3005

[a] projected

[b] including Quebec

When a large number of footnotes are needed, special symbols such as asterisks may be doubled (**) and even tripled (***). Symbols should also be used to indicate notes within the body of mathematical and certain other scientific texts because superscript numerals could be confused with mathematical indices.

9.06   Note content of first reference to a monograph

If it is not included in a bibliography, the source work should be cited in detail the first time it is noted. A detailed footnote or endnote description of a monograph (book) should include the following:

Name of author, editor, compiler or institution responsible
for producing the book
Full title (including subtitle, if any)
Series (if any)
Volume number (if multivolume work)
Edition (if not the first)
Place of publication
Publisher's name
Date of publication
Page number(s) referred to

The first and last words of an English-language title are always capitalized, as are all nouns, pronouns, adjectives, verbs and adverbs. An article, conjunction or preposition (including the *to* in infinitives) is lower-cased unless it is the first or last word of the title or subtitle. (See 4.28 for examples.) The title of a work is italicized in print, underlined in manuscript.

The place of publication, publisher's name and date of publication should be enclosed in parentheses, as in the examples below, but page references should remain outside the parentheses. The author's name is followed by a comma, and the name of the place of publication by a colon and one space. A comma follows the parentheses:

> 1. David C. Neice, *Ethnicity and Canadian Citizenship: A Metropolitan Study* (Ottawa: Supply and Services Canada, 1978), p. 65.

> 2. J. Kage, *With Faith and Thanksgiving* (Montréal: Eagle Publishing Co., 1962), p. 23−46.

If the source material is listed in a bibliography at the end of the text, reference notes may not require elaborate treatment. The first reference to a book should comprise the author's initials and surname, the title of the work, and the relevant page number(s). Out of the comprehensive entry

> 3. Milton M. Gordon, *Assimilation in American Life: The Role of Race, Religion and National Origins* (New York: Oxford University Press, 1964), p. 56.

only the following elements need be retained:

> 4. Milton M. Gordon, *Assimilation in American Life,* p. 56.

9.07 Subsequent references

Second and subsequent references to a work may be shorter still. Only the last name of the author, key word(s) in the title, and the page number(s) are required. Thus the entry for Neice is reduced to

> 5. Neice, *Ethnicity,* p. 112.

If only one work—monograph or article—by the author concerned is quoted, her or his name and the page number(s) will suffice.

9.08 Note content for articles

Information in a note reference to a periodical or journal article should include the name of the author(s), the title of the article, the name of the periodical or journal, the volume and issue numbers, the date and the page number(s), as exemplified in the following:

> 1. George E. Wilson, "New Brunswick's Entrance into Confederation," *Canadian Historical Review,* 10, 1 (March 1928): 23–24.

> 2. R. G. Berry, "Manpower Needs in Psychological Services in Ontario 1965–1970," *Ontario Psychological Quarterly,* 17 (Summer 1965): 45.

Note that the article title is enclosed in double quotation marks and the periodical title italicized (underlined in manuscripts). The date is placed in parentheses and no comma separates it from the volume and issue numbers. In accordance with International Standard ISO 690-1975, the abbreviation *p.* or *pp.* may be omitted. A colon then precedes the page number(s). However, if the volume number has not been given, the abbreviation is used and is preceded by a comma:

> 3. W. Epstein, "Canada's Disarmament Initiatives Mark Return to Active Role," *International Perspectives* (March–April, 1979), p. 8.

References to scientific periodicals have a special format (see 9.15).

9.09 Newspapers and magazines

References to newspapers and magazines require the name of the writer (if given), article title, name of the publication, date of issue and page number. The name of a newspaper should be given as it appears on the masthead. If the city name does not appear there, give it in square brackets after the name:

> 11. Kathryn May, "Soil Erosion Will Cause Food Shortages: Report," *The Citizen* [Ottawa], July 17, 1984, p. 4.

> 12. Peter Lewis, "A Prescription for Anarchy in Europe," *Maclean's,* July 16, 1984, p. 40.

9.10 Corporate author

Documents that do not have a specified author or editor, such as government publications or proceedings of parliamentary committees, should be footnoted under the title of the sponsoring body, which may be a country, its legislative body, or a department, board, agency or commission, a province or municipality, an association or a company:

> 17. Canada, House of Commons, *Debates,* December 8, 1975, p. 43–45.

> 18. Statistics Canada, *Advanced Statistics of Education 1975–1976* (Ottawa, 1975), p. 43–49.

References to parliamentary documents such as committee papers and Hansard need not include volume and number; the date is sufficient identification, particularly if the document is listed subsequently in a bibliography.

9.11   Author-date system

One alternative to footnotes and endnotes is to identify the source material within the body of the text simply by name of author and date of publication, as illustrated below:

> The dominance of English as the language of the higher levels of business in Quebec is determined by the international status of English (*lingua franca*), which is reinforced by the close ties of the Quebec economy to the rest of English-speaking Canada, the recent presence of American multinational firms in Quebec, and the importance of English-speaking entrepreneurs and financiers in the economic development of Quebec (Breton and Mieszkowski 1975, 1977; Faucher and Lamontagne 1953; Morrison 1970; Simon 1974).

Full bibliographical entries for the authors concerned are then given in a reference list at the end of the text, as illustrated:

> Breton, Albert and Peter Mieszkowski.
>
> 1975   "The Returns to Investment in Language: The Economics of Bilingualism." Discussion Paper No. 7512. Toronto: University of Toronto.
>
> 1977   "The Economics of Bilingualism." In *The Political Economy of Fiscal Federalism. International Institute of Management,* edited by Wallace E. Oates. Lexington, Mass: Lexington Books, p. 261–73.

The bibliography is arranged in alphabetical order of the authors' names and chronologically for the works of each author. Where reference is made to two or more works published by an author in the same year, references are assigned letters:

> Lupul 1978*a*
>
> Lupul 1978*b*

9.12   Author-number system

Another alternative, the author-number system, involves not an alphabetical but a numerical arrangement of bibliographical references. Within the body of the text the writer merely cites the name of the author of each source work along with a key number in parentheses on the same line:

> A fundamental strategic problem is to appraise the feasibility of conducting an outcome evaluation. Boruch (2) has discussed the importance of so doing. . . .

In the accompanying bibliographical reference list, arranged numerically, the first reference to a work contains full details—except in a book with a main bibliography at the end, in which case a shortened note is required—and subsequent notes are as brief as possible, in accordance with the guidelines given in 9.07. The bibliographical entry for the preceding example is

> 2. Boruch, Robert F. *Appropriateness and Feasibility of Randomized Field Tests* (Evaluation Research Program Document C-21). Unpublished manuscript, Northwestern University, 1976.

The advantage of the author-number system is that footnotes are required only for comments by the writer, examples and allusions. The inherent difficulty is that the writer must keep a running list of source works and appropriate page numbers at the first draft stage, in order to ensure that each work is assigned the same number in every pertinent note reference.

9.13 Reference note abbreviations

Many scientific publications and other scholarly or technical works have abbreviations in their notes. One obvious reason for this is that, in a text containing a significant number of references, abbreviations help keep the notes as short as possible. Clarity should not be sacrificed to conciseness, however. For the reader's benefit, abbreviation lists may be given at the beginning of a book or article.

9.14 Legal references

Legal references require a more elaborate note system than more general works and government publications. The most evident difference is that lawyers and legal scholars adopt many abbreviations in their references. Use these abbreviations if the intended reader has specialized knowledge of the legal field, but use only familiar abbreviations when writing for a general audience.

Monographs. Books on legal topics may be presented in the same format as works in the humanities. However, because of the many footnotes in legal writing, legal specialists tend to omit the author's initial, place of publication and publisher's name in order to save space:

> 1. Linden, *Canadian Negligence Law* (1972), at 259.

Note the use of "at" in legal references. The abbreviation *p.* or *pp.* may be dropped in the interest of brevity.

Articles. Provide information in the following order: surname of author, title of article in quotation marks, year of publication in parentheses, periodical volume number, abbreviated periodical title in quotation marks (in italics in the *Supreme Court Reports*), the number of the first page of the article, and the actual reference page number:

> 2. Castel, "Some Legal Aspects of Human Organ Transplantation in Canada," (1968) 46 "Can. Bar Rev." 345, at 361.

Judgments. For volumes of the *Supreme Court Reports* from 1923 on, give the case name in italics, followed by a comma, the year of publication in brackets, the issue number (if desired), the abbreviation for the Reports, the number of the first page of the judgment, and the reference page number:

> 3. *Higgins v. Comox Logging and Ry. Co.,* [1927] 1 S.C.R. 359, at 360.

For volumes prior to 1923, cite the case name in italics and the year the judgment was rendered in parentheses, followed by a comma, the volume number, the abbreviation for the Reports, and the number of the first page of the citation:

> 4. *Burland v. Moffat* (1885), 11 S.C.R. 76.

For the *Federal Court Reports* use the same format as for post-1922 S.C.R. volumes:

> 5. *Canadian Pacific Air Lines, Limited v. The Queen,* [1979] 1 F.C. 39, at 40.

For the *Dominion Law Reports* give the case name in italics and, if desired, the date of judgment in parentheses before the comma, the volume number, the abbreviation for the Reports, the series number in parentheses, the number of the first page of the judgment, the reference page number and, if desired, the abbreviation for the court in parentheses:

> 6. *Beim v. Goyer* (1966), 57 D.L.R. (2d) 253, at 256 (S.C.C.).

The reference is complete without the date; the reader could find Volume 57 of the second series without knowing the date of judgment, which is therefore an optional addition for information purposes alone. However, there is an alternative D.L.R. format which incorporates a date as part of the reference:

> 7. *Nova Mink v. TCA,* [1951] 2 D.L.R. 241, at 254 (N.S.C.A.).

Here the date, which is the date of publication and therefore not necessarily the date of judgment, is in effect part of the volume number, while the number following it is that of the issue.

Statutes. When an Act is mentioned in a text, it is helpful to provide a footnote indicating the chapter of the *Revised Statutes of Canada, Statutes of Canada* or provincial statutes where the Act may be found and listing the number of the section containing the relevant information:

> 8. R.S.C. 1970, c. E-10, s. 5.

> 9. R.S.O. 1980, c. 228, s. 10.

International agreements. Give the title of the agreement, treaty or convention, place and date of signature, place of publication, publisher's name, and date of publication:

> 10. Universal Copyright Convention, Geneva, September 6, 1952. London: HMSO, 1952.

9.15 Scientific publications: presentation of articles

Endnote, footnote and bibliographical entries for articles in specialized periodicals in the natural, applied and social sciences are generally treated differently:

only the first word of the article title and proper names and their derivatives are capitalized;

since most scientific publications use the author-date system in references, the date of publication is placed directly after or below the author's name;

no quotation marks are used for the title of the article;

the title of the publication is invariably abbreviated and in many cases not italicized;

the volume or issue number is followed by a colon, and *p.* or *pp.* is not used.

The following examples illustrate these points:

> Ivan, M., and M. Hidiroglou. 1980. The Ottawa plastic metabolism cage for sheep. Can. J. Anim. Sci. 60: 539–41.

> Steel, C.G.H.; G.P. Morris. 1977. A simpie technique for selective staining of neurosecretory products in epoxy section with paraldehyde fuchsin. Can. J. Zool. 55: 1571–75.

9.16 Abbreviation of titles of periodicals

Guidelines for the creation of title abbreviations for serial and non-serial publications are provided in ISO International Standard 4-1972, *Documentation—International Code for the Abbreviation of Titles of Periodicals.* Extensive lists of abbreviations may be found in the above standard, in the *World List of Scientific Periodicals,* and in the *Bibliographic Guide for Editors and Authors.*

The following is a list of abbreviations for words commonly found in scientific periodical titles. The abbreviations of the names of subject fields are also used for the adjectives derived therefrom. Note that monosyllabic words are not abbreviated.

Abstr.	Abstract(s)	Biochem.	Biochemistry
Adv.	Advance(s)	Biol.	Biology
Alm.	Almanac	Br.	British
Am.	American	Cal.	Calendar
Annu.	Annual	Can.	Canadian
Appl.	Applied	Chem.	Chemistry
Astron.	Astronomy	Chron.	Chronicle(s)
Astrophys.	Astrophysics	Circ.	Circular
At.	Atomic	Comm.	Communication(s)
Atmos.	Atmospheric	Comput.	Computational
Bibliogr.	Bibliography	Contr.	Contribution(s)

Cour.	Courier	Obs.	Observations
Cryst.	Crystal	Opt.	Optical
Crystallogr.	Crystallography	Org.	Organic
Dig.	Digest	Pap.	Papers
Dyn.	Dynamics	Philos.	Philosophy
Electr.	Electrical	Phys.	Physics
Electrochem.	Electrochemistry	Physiol.	Physiology
Electron.	Electronic	Planet.	Planetary
Eng.	Engineering	Polym.	Polymer
Exp.	Experimental	Proc.	Proceedings
For.	Forest(ry)	Prog.	Progress
Gen.	General	Publ.	Publication(s)
Genet.	Genetics	Q.	Quarterly
Geophys.	Geophysics	Radiat.	Radiation
Ill.	Illustrated	Rec.	Record(s)
Ind.	Industrial	Ref.	Reference
Inf.	Information	Rep.	Report(s)
Inorg.	Inorganic	Res.	Research(es)
Int.	International	Rev.	Review(s)
J.	Journal	Russ.	Russian
Lett.	Letters	Sci.	Science(s)
Mag.	Magazine	Ser.	Series
Magn.	Magnetic	Soc.	Society
Mater.	Material(s)	Sol.	Solar
Math.	Mathematics	Spectros.	Spectroscopy
Med.	Medical	Stand.	Standard(s)
Mem.	Memoirs	Stat.	Statistics
Met.	Metal	Sov.	Soviet
Metall.	Metallurgy	Tech.	Technical,
Mech.	Mechanics		Techniques
Misc.	Miscellany	Technol.	Technology
Mol.	Molecular	Theor.	Theoretical
Mon.	Monthly	Trans.	Transactions
Microbiol.	Microbiology	Transl.	Translation
Nat.	National	Zool.	Zoology
Natl.	Nature, Natural		

The abbreviated titles of some Canadian journals are presented below as an illustration:

C.J. Biochem.	Canadian Journal of Biochemistry
Can. J. Chem.	Canadian Journal of Chemistry
Can. J. Chem. Eng.	Canadian Journal of Chemical Engineering
Can. J. Earth Sci.	Canadian Journal of Earth Sciences
Can. J. For. Res.	Canadian Journal of Forest Research
Can. J. Microbiol.	Canadian Journal of Microbiology
Can. J. Neurol. Sci.	Canadian Journal of Neurological Sciences
Can. J. Soil Sci.	Canadian Journal of Soil Science
Can. J. Zool.	Canadian Journal of Zoology

Bibiliographies

9.17 Types of bibliography

Various types of bibliography are possible, depending on the nature of the book or document in which they are to appear. A bibliography may list all the works consulted in writing the text as well as others the writer believes the reader will find useful, or it may be restricted to a listing of works actually cited in the text (a **list of works cited** or **selected bibliography)**. An **annotated bibliography** will contain comments by the author concerning the scope, the usefulness or other features of the works listed. Works on scientific or technical subjects often have a **reference list** instead of a bibliography, with a somewhat different treatment of the basic bibliographical information (see 9.15).

The bibliography normally appears at the end of a book, report or other document, before the index (if any). When each chapter has a separate bibliography, however, it should appear immediately after the chapter in question.

9.18 Arrangement

If a book covers a broad subject, or if each chapter in it is devoted to a different topic, it may be more practical to break the source material down into a general bibliography of works covering the subject as a whole and a number of separate listings of works referring to specific chapter topics or fields. *The Canada Year Book,* for example, contains a listing of general reference works followed by a number of separate listings for fine arts and performing arts, linguistics and literature, economics, government and law, religion, science and technology, and so on. Other arrangements are possible—separate listings for monographs and articles, for example. In most cases, however, a straightforward alphabetical, letter-by-letter arrangement will suffice (see 9.39). Choose an arrangement that presents the source works in as clear, orderly and logical a manner as possible.

9.19 Composition of monograph entry

The following items, as applicable, are required in a monograph entry: name of author (editor, compiler, or institution responsible for producing the work); title and subtitle; series; volume number, edition (if not the first); place of publication; publisher; and date of publication. The physical facts about a work—number of pages, number of illustrations, plates and so on—can be omitted, unless they are considered an important feature of the work. See International Standard ISO 690–1975 for further information.

As in the case of footnotes, titles are normally italicized in print, but can simply be underlined in manuscripts if it is more convenient to do so:

> McConnell, Ruth E. *Our Own Voice: Canadian English and How It Came to Be.* Toronto: Gage, 1978.

Note, in the example, the indention of the second line, the periods after the author's name and the title, the capitalization procedures (the same as for notes), and the colon followed by a single space after the place of publication. Copy a title exactly from the title page of the publication and, when no punctuation separates the main title and subtitle on the title page, insert a colon or, if necessary, a period after the main title in the bibliographical entry. The author's surname precedes the given name and initials.

The date of publication of some books cannot be ascertained from the book itself. In such cases, enter the copyright date or check library records for the missing information.

9.20 Composition of article entry

The entry for an article in a journal comprises the following: author's name, title of the article, name of the periodical, volume and issue number, date, and the pages taken up by the article. As with monographs, the author's name is inverted and the article title is enclosed in quotation marks and followed by a period inside the closing quotation marks:

> Palmer, Sally. "The Role of the Social Worker in Provincial Psychiatric Hospitals: An Ontario Study." *Canada's Mental Health,* 32, 4 (December 1984): 8–11.

Note that when no volume number is given, page references are identified by *p.* or *pp.* Note also that many specialized scientific journals require the volume number to be in Arabic numerals, even if the periodical in the bibliographical entry uses Roman numerals on its cover.

Periodical titles may be abbreviated in standard ways (see 9.16), but this should not be done if there is doubt as to whether the reader will be familiar with the abbreviated titles.

9.21 Order of precedence in alphabetical arrangement

Note the following conventions concerning alphabetical order of bibliographical entries:

- a single-author entry precedes a multiple-author entry beginning with the same name;
- an author's own volume precedes one that he or she has edited or compiled;
- corporate authors are alphabetized according to the first key word in the name;
- a list of works by the same author is presented in chronological order.

In addition, the rules given below (9.39, 9.42–9.47) for alphabetizing index entries also apply to bibliographical entries.

9.22 Examples of specific entries

Multiple-author entry. Note that the second author's name does not have to be inverted:

> Morris, Raymond N., and C. Michael Lanphier. *Three Scales of Inequality: Perspectives on French-English Relations.* Don Mills, Ont.: Longmans Canada, 1977.

For three or more authors, give the principal author's name, followed by *et al.* or *and others:*

> Franck, Thomas M., et al. *Why Federations Fail: An Enquiry into the Requisites for Successful Federalism.* Studies in Peaceful Change, No. 1. New York: New York University Press, 1968.

More than one work by the same author.

> Lijphart, Arend. *The Politics of Accommodation. Pluralism and Democracy in the Netherlands.* Berkeley and Los Angeles: University of California Press, 1968.
>
> ——. *Democracy in Plural Societies: A Comparative Exploration.* New Haven: Yale University Press, 1980.

As shown above, a line or series of dashes may be substituted for the author's name after the first work has been listed.

Governments. Publications of federal, provincial, state and municipal governments are entered under the name of the country, province, state or municipality issuing the document:

> Canada. Department of Industry, Trade and Commerce. *Annual Report, 1975–1976.* Ottawa, 1977.

Since the government or government department is the publisher in such cases, the publisher's name, which normally follows the place of publication, is omitted.

Parliamentary documents should be grouped together under a subheading, as illustrated:

> Canada, Parliament
> > House of Commons. *Debates,* April 30, 1979.
> > ———. *Order Paper and Notices,* May 29, 1978.
> > ———. Standing Committee on Public Accounts,
> > *Minutes of Proceedings and Evidence,* April 6, 1982.
> > Senate. *Minutes of Proceedings,* June 26, 1975.
> > ———. Standing Committee on Foreign Affairs,
> > *Proceedings,* January 22, 1981.

Institutions and corporate bodies. Documents published by universities, museums, libraries and other institutions are entered under the name of the institution or corporate body:

> Community Planning Association of Canada. *Canadian Housing Resource Catalogue.* Ottawa, 1975.

> Metric Commission Canada. Metric Press Guide, 2nd ed. Ottawa, n.d.

> National Film Board of Canada. *A Catalogue of Films Projecting Women.* Toronto, 1975.

> The Canadian Press. *Caps and Spelling,* 6th rev. ed. Toronto, 1981.

> Toronto Public Library. *The Osborne Collection of Early Children's Books, 1476–1910: A Catalogue.* Toronto, 1975.

> University of Kentucky. *The University of Kentucky: Its History and Development.* Lexington, 1950.

International bodies. Such bodies are listed under the name of the organization:

> North Atlantic Treaty Organization. *Annual Report, 1975.* Brussels, *1976.*

> United Nations Statistical Office. *Yearbook of International Trade Statistics, 1952.* New York, 1953.

Conference proceedings. These are identified by conference title:

> *Human Translation : Machine Translation.* Papers from the Tenth Annual Conference on Computational Linguistics, Odense, November 22–23, 1979. Vienna: Infoterm, 1980.

9.23 Editors, compilers and translators

Where the name under which a work is listed is in fact that of an editor, compiler or translator, the abbreviation *ed., comp.,* or *transl.* should follow the name in the bibliographical entry:

> Hindley, Geoffrey, ed. *The Larousse Encyclopedia of Music.* London: Hamlyn Publishing Group, 1975.

> Johnsen, Julia E., comp. *Federal Price Control.* New York: Wilson, 1942.

> Pawley, Arthur, transl. *More Translations from the Arabic.* London: Blackman, 1951.

A work frequently used for reference, however, is often entered by the title, whether or not the editor or compiler is named on the title page:

> *Dictionary of Canadian Biography.* Edited by George W. Brown. Toronto: University of Toronto Press, 1966.

When both the author's and the editor's (or translator's) names are given, the editor's (or translator's) name is set off by periods:

> Pearson, Lester B. *Mike: The Memoirs of the Right Honourable Lester B. Pearson,* Vol. 3, 1957–1968. Edited by John A. Munro and Alex I. Inglis. Toronto: University of Toronto Press, 1975.

The title of an article or essay in a collection of pieces by several different authors or by the same author is printed in roman type between quotation marks and followed by a period. The title of the volume is then given in italics, preceded by *In.* The page references for the article or essay in question follow the publishing data:

> Orwell, George. "Politics and the English Language." In Contemporary Essays. Edited by Donald R. Nickerson. Boston: Ginn and Co., 1965, p. 303–315.

9.24 Translation and transliteration

A title in one of the more familiar European languages is not usually translated unless the translated title appears on the title page. When it does, the English version of the title follows the primary title in the bibliographical entry and is underlined without brackets. If you have to supply a translation, insert the English version of the title in brackets, not underlined and with only the initial word capitalized, after the primary title. If brackets are not used, place a period after both titles; if they are, place a period after the translation and no punctuation at all after the primary title. For a publication in which French and English titles are given, both languages should be included:

> Norway. Statistisk sentralbyraa. *Husholdnings regnskaper for alderstrygdede, Mai 1955–April 1956. Family Budgets for Old Age Pensioners, May 1955–April 1956.* Oslo, 1958.

> Karcsay, Simon. *Jogi es allamigazgatasi szotar* [Vocabulary of law and administration]. Munich: Beck, 1969.

> Art Gallery of Ontario. *Exposure: Canadian Contemporary Photographers / Exposure: photographes canadiens contemporains.* Toronto, 1975.

Titles and authors' names in languages that do not use Roman script are transliterated according to an internationally recognized system and then translated. Transliteration guidelines may be found in the relevant ISO standards, the *MLA Handbook* and the *Anglo-American Cataloguing Rules.* If the title in English appears on the title page, it is entered immediately following the transliterated title. If it does not, the English translation is placed between brackets:

> China. National Tariff Commission. *Shang-hai wu chia nien kan, 1938. An Annual Report of Shanghai Commodity Prices, 1938.* Peking, n.d.

> Zuraig, Qustantin. *Ma na an-Nakba* [The meaning of the disaster]. Beirut: Dar al-Ilm lil-Malayin, 1948.

The publisher's name should not be translated, but for the benefit of the unilingual reader the place of publication may be.

When no translation is given on the title page, check whether translations of the work are already on record at the National Library, the Canadian Institute for Scientific and Technical Information or elsewhere before having the primary title translated. Accuracy of translation is essential.

9.25 Unpublished works

For most kinds of unpublished material, the arrangement of information used is generally the same as for published works:

> Wood, Cecil G. *"Creacionismo* or the Search for the Absolute in the Poetry of Vicente Huidobro." Ph.D. dissertation, University of Toronto, 1974.

Note that the thesis title is placed in quotation marks.

9.26 Pseudonymous or anonymous works

Authors better known by a pseudonym than by their real name should be listed under the pseudonym. The real name may be given in brackets after the pseudonym; if the author's real name is not known, *pseud.* may be given in brackets after the pseudonym. If the author of an anonymous work has been established, her or his name is given in brackets. If not, the work is listed simply by its title. The use of *anonymous* or *anon.* should be avoided:

> Carroll, Lewis [Charles Lutwidge Dodgson]. *Through the Looking Glass.* New York: Random House, 1946.

> [Horsley, Samuel]. *On the Prosodies of the Greek and Latin Languages.* 1796.

> "Summer is Icumen In." In *Immortal Poems of the English Language.* Edited by Oscar Williams. New York: Pocket Books, 1954.

9.27 Non-print media

Lectures. Give the speaker's name, the title of the lecture in quotation marks, the sponsoring organization, the location and the date:

> Landry, Alain. "The Size of the Task or If You Have Problems." Seminar: "The Challenge of Canada's French Language Market," Canadian Manufacturers' Association (CMA), Toronto, November 28, 1978.

Films. Include the title (underlined or italicized), distributor and date, along with any other pertinent information. It may, for example, be convenient to list the entry under the director's name:

> Brittain, Donald and John Kramer, dirs. *Volcano: An Inquiry into the Life and Death of Malcolm Lowry.* Richard Burton narrates Lowry's letters and excerpts from his works. National Film Board of Canada, 1976.

Theatrical performances. In addition to the items listed in a film entry, give the theatre, city and date of performance, along with any other information deemed pertinent:

> Millerd, Bill, dir. *Rexy!* By Allan Stratton. With Enid Simpson. Phoenix Theatre, Toronto, 1981.

Musical recordings. Give the name of the composer, the title of the recording (or the works on the recording), artist's name, manufacturer, catalogue number and year of issue, and any other pertinent information:

> Somers, Harry. *The Fool.* With Roxolana Roslak, Patricia Rideout, David Astor, Maurice Brown. Cond. Victor Feldbrill, RCA, LSC 3094 (CBC, 272), n.d.

Radio and television programs. List the entry under the title of the program and include the network or local station, the city and the date of broadcast, together with other pertinent information:

> *The Golden Triangle: Canada's Heroin Connection.* Narr. George McLean. Continuity writ. Robert Gardiner. Research by Pat Graham. Prod. and dir. by Robert D. Clark. CBC Ottawa Film Production. February 23, 1984.

Personal and telephone interviews. Enter the interviewee, the mode of communication and the date:

> Vonnegut, Kurt. Personal interview. July 27, 1976.

Audiotapes and videotapes from documentation services. List the entry under the name of the organization if there is no specified author, and state the type of recording:

> Manitoba. Department of Highways and Transportation. Motor Vehicle Branch. *Manitoba Drivers Handbook,* audiotape. Winnipeg, 1980.

> University of Toronto. *The Canadian General Career of Sir William Otter, 1860–1921,* videocassette. Distributed by University of Toronto, Toronto, 1975.

9.28   Common abbreviations in notes and bibliographies

Abbreviations can help make your footnotes, endnotes and bibliographical entries more concise. For lists of relevant abbreviations see International Standard ISO 832, *Documentation—Bibliographical References—Abbreviations of Typical Words,* and the 1984 edition of the *MLA Handbook.*

Indexes

9.29   Definition

An index is a systematic guide to significant items or concepts mentioned or discussed in a work or group of works; the items and concepts are represented by a series of entries arranged in a known or searchable order, with a **locator,** which is an indication of the place(s) in the work(s) where reference to each item or concept may be found.

9.30   Scope and complexity

An index may be **general** or **specific.** A **general** one lists subjects, authors, persons or corporate bodies, geographical names and other items. A **specific** index is limited to a particular category of entry, such as one of the items in the above list, abbreviations and acronyms, or citations.

A work may contain a general index and one or more specific indexes. The *Dictionary of Canadian Biography,* for example, has three: an index of identifications (occupational sectors of those listed), a geographical index and a nominal index. Multiple listings are designed to help readers research a particular aspect of the subject concerned.

The complexity of indexing has fostered the development of a number of computerized indexing methods (see bibliography). Human intervention is nonetheless required in many aspects of hierarchical arrangement, alphabetization, choice of terms, word order, capitalization and cross-referencing.

9.31 Arrangement

The order of entries is usually alphabetical, and each entry is followed by a locator. The arrangement may vary, however, depending on the contents of the work being indexed. A chronological arrangement would be suitable for an index of historical events and persons, for example, and a numerical one might be required for lists of chemical elements, patents or highways.

9.32 Length

Agreement must be reached beforehand with the publisher on the length of the index. Normally, an index should not exceed five percent of the number of pages in the work itself. The need for completeness should be tempered by consideration of the extent of the prospective reader's knowledge of the subject matter.

9.33 Referenced material

Do not index the title page of a work, its table of contents and dedication, epigraphs, abstracts of articles, or synopses at the beginning of chapters. Include references to illustrations, photographs, graphs, tables and figures only if they give pertinent information not provided in the body of the text.

On the other hand, the index should, in addition to the text proper, cover introductions, addenda, appendixes and substantive notes, forewords and prefaces that contain pertinent information, and—in the case of newspapers and periodicals—book reviews and letters to the editor.

9.34 Simple entry

A **simple entry** is composed of an **identifier**, which is the heading, and a **locator**—the page or section number(s) etc. where reference to the item may be found:

Dominion Fire Commissioner, 911

Drainage basins, 4–6

Drugs, control of, 180–82

Duties, customs and excise, 802, 812, 818, 824

Each item is listed according to the key word, so inversion of phrases is often necessary, with a comma separating the two elements of the inversion. The full heading is followed by a comma. The page numbers are given without *p.* or *pp.,* and inclusive numbers should be presented in accordance with the rules enunciated in 5.24, e.g. 47–48, 101–106, 213–18, 1653–1703. Avoid the use of *f., ff.* and *et seq.* in place of numerals.

9.35 Complex entry

A **complex entry** is composed of a main entry (with a main heading) and one or more subentries (subheadings), each with a locator. The complex entry may be presented in run-in or indent format:

run-in	**indent**
Maritimes, English in, 21, 32, 39; French in, 80; surveys in, 119	Maritimes, English in, 21, 32, 39 French in, 80 surveys in, 119

The two formats reflect the same inverted word order, a comma follows the heading in each case, and the second and subsequent lines of the entry are indented. In the run-in format, however, the entry is presented in paragraph style, with each subentry being followed by a semicolon. In the indent format the presentation is columnar: the main entry and each subentry stand on a separate line, so semicolons are not required. In neither case does a period close the entry.

The advantage of the run-in format is that it saves space and can provide a seminarrative, chronological outline of events in a biographical or historical context, as shown in the following listing for a Canadian ship that was engaged in action in World War II:

Haida, 197, 250; action of April 26/44, 251; action of April
    29/44, 253, 258; 266; action of June 9/44, 286, 300;
    U-boat kill, 302; Channel and Biscay actions, 340, 348,
    359, 401, 406

The advantage of the indent format is that it is more legible and makes the relationships between items more readily apparent to the reader. Use it when such relationships are to be highlighted, as in the case of scientific indexes:

Muscles, skeletal
    congenital defects of, 342
    contracture of, 326
    diseases of, 226
    dystrophy of, 326, 896
        enzootic, 893, 896, 1015
        foals, 424
    hypertrophy, inherited, 1052

The example, taken from the field of veterinary medicine, illustrates the use of sub-subentries. In such circumstances a columnar presentation is essential.

9.36 Choice of terms

The wording of the entry should be as specific as possible for the prospective reader's purposes. Popular or specialized terms may be used, depending on the reader and the nature of the work. When preparing an index, you can glean established nomenclature from the indexes of previous publications on the same subject or from thesauri, or you can create your own headings on the basis of the work at hand. In doing so, check the author's terms for consistency and accuracy and, if necessary, use a standard term instead.

9.37   Syntax of heading

Definite and indefinite articles, adverbs, and finite and infinitive verbs should not be included in headings or subheadings except in the case of headings comprising titles of works of art. The only verb form permitted is the gerund. Retain conjunctions and prepositions essential to establishing a semantic link within the headings. Some latitude is possible here, however. Note that there is no prepositional link between the heading "Muscles, skeletal" (see 9.35 above) and the subheading "hypertrophy, inherited"; the reader will understand the semantic relationship between the two items, and the columnar presentation clearly shows that one is an aspect of the other.

In determining the word order of a heading, the first step is to select a key word or phrase under which to list the entry. For example, an indexable subject in a social science manual might be the sources and collection of statistical data. *Statistical data* would be the key term and the entry would appear thus:

Statistical data, sources and collection of, 57

Sources and collection cannot be used as a key phrase because it is not specific enough. Accordingly, the normal word order has to be inverted and a comma is required after the key phrase. Inversion serves to reduce scattering of related headings and page numbers throughout an index because headings with the same key word will be located close together, e.g. *Heating, electric* and *Heating, oil-fired.*

An action word (gerund) in a heading is normally brought to the fore if the entry is listed under a noun:

Mean, determining standard error of, 35

In the interest of brevity, however, the gerund in the above example could be dropped, since the reader will realize what is entailed in the reference.

Another way of achieving conciseness is to drop prepositions. In the following example, the key phrase is followed by a logical sequence of modifiers:

Copper ores, mining, grinding, screening, pulverizing and
     floating

With the key phrase in boldface type, the preposition *of* can be dropped without causing the reader any problems of comprehension.

An adjective is inverted unless it is part of a name and the noun itself is non-specific:

Oral cavity

Pulmonary disease

9.38 Entry v. subentry

The indexer is constantly faced with the problem of whether to list references to a topic in a series of simple entries or as one main entry with a number of subentries. For example, references to the various types of statistical mean are scattered through a statistical work. They could be indexed in one large, complex entry:

Mean
   arithmetic, 28,
      for grouped data, 29, 135
      properties of, 29, 136–37
   geometric, 31,
      for chained ratios, 32, 138
      properties of, 31, 139–41
   harmonic, 32, 142

Since the document is a specialized one, however, it makes more sense to create main entries for each type of mean, with a cross-reference (see 9.49) from *Mean,* thereby obviating the need for sub-subentries and the repetition of page number references.

In general, avoid single subentries and sub-subentries. In the interest of conciseness, the complex entry

Spasticity
   neonatal, inherited, 1046
   periodic, inherited, 1046

can easily be reduced to

Spasticity, inherited neonatal and periodic, 1046

9.39 Alphabetical arrangement

Headings may be alphabetized letter by letter or word by word:

letter by letter	word by word
Laurence, Margaret	Laurence, Margaret
Leacock, Stephen	Le Jeune, Père
Leechman, Douglas	Le Pan, Douglas
Le Jeune, Père	Leacock, Stephen
Le Pan, Douglas	Leechman, Douglas

In the word-by-word listing, the position of the two-word names is determined by the first word; the second part of the surname comes into play in determining which of the two names is listed first. In the letter-by-letter arrangement, the number of words in the heading is irrelevant.

Use the letter-by-letter format for an index of acronyms, letters and symbols with technical meanings, as in a scientific work.

List organizations by their acronyms or abbreviations if they are usually referred to thereby. The short form should be alphabetized letter by letter and followed immediately by the full title in parentheses or a cross-reference from that title.

A word-for-word arrangement is often used in a proper noun listing of geographical names:

North Umpqua	Northumberland Strait
North Valley Stream	Northumbria
North Vancouver	Northvale
North Vernon	Northville
North Versailles	

In a letter-by-letter listing, the entries with the word *North* would not have been grouped together.

The word-by-word listing provides for a clear grouping of related headings—e.g. *book, book jacket, book label* and *book list,* which would otherwise be separated by a heading such as *bookkeeping.* Its disadvantage is that a related term may have to be separated from the grouping because it is one word, hyphenated or unhyphenated. For example, words such as *booklet* and *bookmark* might well be separated from the above group, even though they belong to the same subject field. This shows the advantage of a letter-by-letter listing: a compound occupies the same position, whether it is unhyphenated, hyphenated or written as two words.

Note that, whichever arrangement is adopted, prepositions at the beginning of a subentry or sub-subentry must be disregarded for alphabetization purposes.

9.40   Listing of subentries

Subentries are generally listed in alphabetical order of the first noun in the subheading, but a chronological, mathematical or other listing may be appropriate, as in the case of popes, kings, element numbers in chemistry, geological eras and highway numbers. See 9.35 for an example of chronological listing in a historical work.

9.41   Capitalization

The first letter of a main heading is capitalized, except in certain French and foreign names, the names of chemical compounds with an italicized prefix, and standard symbols with a lower-case first letter:

> van Willebrand disease
> *p*-Aminobenzoic acid
> pH

In scientific texts it is important to distinguish between common and proper nouns. The first letter of a generic or family name in biology is capitalized, but that of a specific epithet or common name is not:

> spirochetes
> Sporotrichinaceae
> *Sporotrichum schenkii*

9.42　Personal names

When an article or preposition is part of an English name, it is alphabetized without inversion, *e.g. de la Roche, Mazo; De Quincey, Thomas*. Names beginning with *Mac, Mc or M'* are alphabetized as if spelled *Mac*. Ignore the apostrophe in treating an Irish name such as *O'Flynn*; alphabetize it as if it were one unpunctuated word.

French surnames beginning with an article or a contraction of an article and a preposition are listed without inversion, e.g. *Le Rouge, Gustave; Du Pont, Georges*. Similarly, names beginning with *d'* are generally not inverted, e.g. *d'Arcy, Jules*. There is no standard method for alphabetizing names beginning with *de* or *de la*. Adopt the personal preference of the individual concerned or the traditional presentation of his or her name, e.g. *Balzac, Honoré de; La Fontaine, Jean de*. Christian saints should be alphabetized by their given names, with an identifier added if necessary:

> John, Saint
>
> John Chrysostom, Saint
>
> John of the Cross, Saint

The choice between *Saint-* and *St-* and between *Sainte-* and *Ste-* in personal names depends on the traditionally preferred presentation. When an abbreviated form is used, it should be alphabetized as if spelled out.

For detailed information on the presentation of English, French and foreign-language names, see the *Anglo-American Cataloguing Rules*.

9.43　Government departments and agencies

Invert the titles of government departments, e.g. *Justice, Department of.* It may be necessary to include a general cross-reference from *Department* informing the reader that each department is listed under the name of the field for which it is responsible.

Sometimes it is worth adding a geographical identifier in parentheses for the sake of clarity:

> Sociedad Nacional de Mineria (Cuba)
>
> Sociedad Nacional de Mineria (Peru)

9.44　Geographical names

Geographical names are alphabetized according to the main noun (*Ontario, Lake; Robson, Mt.*), except where the generic noun is part of the title (*Lake of the Woods*). Non-English names are alphabetized under the article if there is one (*La Prairie; La Tuque; Los Angeles*), but English names with articles are listed under the main noun (*Eastern Townships, The; Pas, The*).

Items are listed under the names most commonly or officially used or most recently adopted, with a cross-reference from the alternative or former title:

> Dahomey. *See* Benin
>
> Rhodesia. *See* Zambia; Zimbabwe

For information about the official versions of Canadian place names, see Appendix I, "Geographical Names."

The English version of a foreign place name should be used. When there are two non-English names for the same place, use the one more commonly found in written English, e.g. *Louvain,* not *Leuwen.*

In the English-speaking world the same name is used for many geographical entities. Use modifiers in parentheses when necessary:

> Hull (Quebec)
>
> Paris (Ontario)

The same word may be listed several times:

> Québec (city)
>
> Quebec (government)
>
> Quebec (province)

In listing the numbers of the pages where reference to a place may be found, remember that the place may often be referred to in the text by its generic noun alone—*the lake, the mountain,* etc.—and that such references should be included in the index entry.

9.45 Newspapers and periodicals

English-language newspapers should be listed under the name of the place of publication if it is part of the title and, if not, under the first word of the title after the definite article, e.g. *Winnipeg Free Press, The.* French-language and foreign-language newspapers are listed under the first noun, e.g. *Journal de Montréal, Le.* The article may be dropped unless the omission will cause difficulty or will appear curious, as in the case of *Devoir, Le.*

Periodicals are listed under their full title, without the article, e.g. *Canadian Journal of Chemistry.* In periodical citation indexes the abbreviated forms of titles are used (see 9.16).

9.46 Scientific names

Arabic numerals, Greek letters, capital letters with a special meaning, and modifiers prefixed to the names of chemical compounds should be disregarded for alphabetization purposes unless they constitute the only difference between entries:

> *N*-Acryloneuraminic acid
>
> *O*-Acryloneuraminic acid

When a Greek letter stands by itself as a separate entry, romanize it, e.g. *Pi, Gamma.*

Abbreviations for scientific terms should generally not be used at the beginning of a main entry except (i) in a cross-reference, (ii) as part of the name of an enzyme or compound, or (iii) when more than one species is listed for a biological genus:

i) CO_2 *See* Carbon Dioxide
ii) mRNA, 16, 56
iii) *Ambystonia maculatum,* 15
   A. mexicanum, 17

Generic names in biology should in any case be abbreviated after the main entry and alphabetized by epithet as a space-saving device:

Triticum sp.
   T. aestivium
   T. durum

9.47 Homonyms

Adopt the following order of entry for homonyms—person or organization (forenames precede surnames); place (cities and towns precede administrative areas, which precede physical features); subject; title of publication:

Hull, Robert (hockey player)
Hull, (Quebec)
Hull, population of
Hull, A Short History of

John, Pope
John, Augustus

Within a list of personal names an alphabetical (*John, Pope; John, Saint*), hierarchical (*John, Saint; John, Pope*) or chronological/numerical (*John XXII; John XXIII*) arrangement is possible. The usual hierarchical order is: saints, popes, emperors and empresses, kings and queens, surnames.

Modifiers must be included in parentheses after each common noun in order to distinguish it from its homonyms:

Character (literature)
Character (psychology)

9.48 Abbreviations and other reference tools

References to material not contained within the body of the text, such as bibliographies, glossaries, illustrations and tables, require a locator in letters as well as in numbers. The numeral can be printed in boldface type, while the element in letters is presented in italics, usually as an abbreviation:

367 *bibliogr.*	bibliography	**54** *(fig. 21)*	figure
345 *glos.*	glossary	**68** *(fn. 2)*	footnote
54 *ill.*	illustration	**36** *(hn.)*	headnote
facing **60**	plate		

When more than one significant reference to an item is made on the same page of a text, and each piece of information is useful, the words *bis* (twice) and *ter* (three times) may follow the page number in the index:

War of 1812–14, 78 (*bis*), 87 (*ter*)

In indexing works with many words on a page, make the reader's search for information easier by assigning a letter or number to each part of the page: e.g. in the *Encyclopedia Britannica, a,b,c* and *d* for the top, upper middle, lower middle and bottom of the left column of a page, and *e,f,g* and *h* for the same parts of the right column (*23a, 23b, 23c*, etc.).

All abbreviations and special reference codes should be explained in an introductory note to the index.

9.49 Cross-references

Cross-references are required to guide the reader from a given heading to a related heading which will lead him or her to the information required or to additional information on the same subject. The cross-reference is printed in italics, except when the subject heading referred to is itself normally presented in italics:

Archaisms. *See* Relic forms; Historical forms
Ryan, Claude, 234–65. See also *Devoir, Le*

There are five ways of indicating cross-references: *See, See also, See under, See also under* and *q.v.*

a) *See* immediately follows the heading. No page numbers are given in the entry. A semicolon is used to separate headings if more than one entry is referred to:

Reference matter. *See* Endnotes; Footnotes; Indexes; Bibliographies

It is sometimes impractical to list a whole series of cross-references, however. If so, make a non-specific reference. For example,

Education, Department of. *See under government of appropriate province*

is a more succinct entry than one including the names of all the provinces.

The *See* cross-reference is appropriate in the following situations:

• When there is an acceptable synonym for the heading chosen:

War of 1812–1814. *See* Invasion of Canada

• When an entry is listed under a different letter from the one the reader might expect:

La Mare, Walter de. *See* de la Mare, Walter

• When a person is known by a title or pseudonym as well as by a first name and surname:

Beaverbrook, Lord. *See* Aitken, Max

• To refer the reader to an antonym of the heading he or she has found:

Peace movement. *See* **War, nuclear**

• To refer the reader to a modern or popular term for the same concept:

Abyssinia. *See* **Ethiopia**

Latter-day Saints. *See* **Mormons**

• To refer the reader from a specific to a more general heading required by the nature of the subject field treated in the work. For example, in a chemistry text, an entry under *Algebra* might be too specific, and a cross-reference

Algebra. *See* **Mathematics**

would be used. Conversely, in a work dealing primarily with mathematics, there would be a separate entry for algebra, but chemistry headings would be more general, e.g.:

Organic compounds. *See* **Chemical compounds**

b) *See also* is used when at least one page number is not common to the two entries concerned. It guides the reader to additional information on a subject and is placed after the page numbers:

Coinages, Canadian, 68, 153. *See also* **Slang**

c) *See under* is used to direct the reader to a subentry:

Mandatory supervision. *See under* **National Parole Board**

d) *See also under* is used in the same way as *See also*, except that it refers the reader to a subentry:

New Brunswick, 8, 14, 162, 170. *See also under* **Maritimes**

e) The abbreviation *q.v.* applies to a particular word or expression within a heading or subheading, indicating that it can be turned to as a separate heading in the same index:

Acadians
  settlement of Port-Royal (now Annapolis Royal, *q.v.*),
  116–27, 244–47

9.50 Blind references

Careless editing of indexes can result in circular cross-referencing of the type illustrated below:

Atlantic provinces. *See* **New Brunswick; Newfoundland; Nova Scotia; Prince Edward Island**

Nova Scotia. *See* **Maritimes**

Maritimes. *See* **Atlantic provinces**

Trace all cross-references to ensure that each of them leads the reader to real information.

9.51 Continued headings

Each page of a printed index contains at least two columns of entries. For the reader's benefit, it is important to ensure that a main heading is repeated— Public Works, Department of *(cont.)*—at the top of the right-hand column or of the left-hand column of the next page if further subentries are to be listed.

9.52 "Dangling" entries

The first line of an entry should never be left at the bottom of a column. Any such entries that are found at the proof or galley stage should be placed at the top of the next column at the head of the rest of the entry.

Ten

Letters and memorandums

10

Letters and memorandums

Letters

10.01 Introduction

The following principle applies not only to letters but also to other forms of communication: say what you have to say clearly and succinctly. The layout of the document should be such that the reader can quickly determine who are the sender and intended recipient, when the document was written or sent, what it is about, what the recipient is expected to do about it, and when and how that person is to do it.

10.02 Block style

Letters are laid out in two basic styles or variations thereof: the block style and the indent style. The one recommended by the Canadian government's Treasury Board for administrative correspondence is the block style. (The Board recognizes that the full block style may not be suitable for all types of correspondence.) In it all lines begin flush with the left margin, including the sender's address, the date, the complimentary close and the signature, as illustrated in the example below (10.25).[1]

10.03 Indent style

In the indent style the sender's address, if not given in the letterhead, appears at the top right-hand corner with the date below it. The complimentary close and signature block are at the bottom right. Finally, the first line of each paragraph in the body of the letter is indented.

10.04 Advantage of block style

In the block style, space is saved horizontally because there is no indention of paragraphs. Little time is lost positioning the various parts of the letter; every line begins flush with the left margin.

---

1. The federal government authority for document layout is the Treasury Board, acting through the Federal Identity Program (FIP) in accordance with Chapter 470 (March 1982) of the Board's *Administrative Policy Manual.* Guidelines on layout, paper and envelope size, and related items may be found in the FIP *Design Guide* (1979). At the time of printing, a revised edition of this guide was in preparation. Future recommendations and directives on document layout issued through the FIP will take precedence over recommendations made in this chapter.

10.05 Margins

Margins may be adjusted to some extent to make a short letter appear longer or a long one look shorter. The left margin must be absolutely straight and the right one as straight as possible without splitting words too often. This requires a fairly wide right margin so that long words can be accommodated.

10.06 Punctuation

Punctuation must be consistent throughout the document and should be used only where clarity demands it. A colon is normally used after the salutation (see 10.16), and a comma after the complimentary close.

10.07 Consistency

For uniformity and consistency, put the parts of the letter, as applicable, in the order shown below. Each part will start two to four lines below the preceding part.

10.08 Letterhead

The heading or letterhead identifies the department or agency that produced the letter. The identification of federal organizations and positions in the letterhead should be in accordance with FIP guidelines.

If the sender's address appears in the letterhead, there is no need to repeat it elsewhere. Otherwise, include a return address below the letterhead or below the signature.

10.09 Date

See 5.14 for the representation of dates.

The date appears at the left margin in full block style (see example), but it can be placed on the right-hand side of the page to help fit in all the pieces of information required.

10.10 Delivery (mailing) notation

The logical place for notations such as *Personal*, *Confidential*, *Registered* or *Hand-delivered* is at the left margin, just below the date line, where the reader would probably look first upon opening the letter. Such notations may be typed all in capital letters or with initial capitals and underlining.

10.11 Reference line

The reference line, on the right-hand side of the page, will give the sender's file number and the line below it the recipient's file number, as shown in the example.

10.12　Inside address

Place the recipient's address below the date and at the left margin.

If the communication is to be sent in a window envelope, or if a record of the address is required for future checking in case of delivery problems, the addressee's full address must be used. It is not required in internal or personal mail. The address should be at least two spaces below the letterhead, if there is one, and flush with the left margin, unless it must be moved to fit properly into a window envelope. It should be single-spaced. The postal code should be the last item in the address and be typed on a separate line or else two spaces after the name of the province.

10.13　Official languages in addresses

See the FIP *Design Guide* for detailed information and guidelines on the presentation of addresses in letters and on other stationery. The Guide specifically covers use of the official languages in addresses and makes the following main points:

• Generally, words indicating a type of public thoroughfare such as *Street*, *rue*, *Avenue* or *avenue*, are translated into the other official language because they do not form part of the official name of the thoroughfare.

• When the word is part of the official name of the thoroughfare, e.g. *Avenue* (*1re*, *2e*, etc.), *Chaussée*, *Chemin*, *Montée*, *Circle*, *Square*, *Avenue* (*1st*, *2nd*, etc.), do not translate it.

• Enquiries concerning the official name of a thoroughfare should be directed to the appropriate municipality.

• Where the names of buildings, locations and areas were established by a municipal government and have no official translation, those names should not be translated, e.g. *Les Terrasses de la Chaudière, Place du Portage, Tunney's Pasture, Blackburn Hamlet.*

• The names of provinces and territories are translated as applicable. In English, a comma is used to set off a place name from that of the province or territory (see 7.21).

See Appendix I, "Geographical Names," for further information on the translation and spelling of such names.

10.14　Name of person, title, name of organization

Put the person's name on one line and his or her title and organization on the next line:

　　J. Doe
　　Chief, Co-ordination Division

10.15 Attention line

The attention line indicates a specific person for whose attention the letter is intended. The line therefore begins with *Attention of*, *Attention* or *Attn*. It specifies the intended recipient within the organization when the letter is addressed to the organization or to the intended recipient's chief. Its purpose is to ensure delivery to the proper person. It always begins at the left margin.

10.16 Salutation or greeting

The recipient either will be the person concerned or will direct the letter to that person. When the addressee's sex is not known, give just the initial and surname; if the person's name is not known, use the expression *To whom it may concern* or else omit the salutation completely—a growing practice in business letters.

When the name of the recipient is known the salutation will vary depending upon the person addressed and the nature of the letter. The following are some appropriate salutations for various circumstances:

Sir **or** Dear Sir   (for formal correspondence)
Madam **or** Dear Madam

Dear Mr. **or** Mrs. **or** Miss   (for a more personal letter)
or Ms. Jones

Dear S. Jones   (if sex of recipient is not known)

In block style the salutation begins at the left margin. For the capitalization of the salutation, see 4.30; for its punctuation, see 7.30.

10.17 Subject line

A subject line specifying the topic of the letter or the name of the person concerned may be included. The introductory word *Subject* followed by a colon may be used, but is not really essential. The terms *Re* and *In re* should be reserved for legal correspondence. The subject line is either typed wholly in upper case or is underlined. It may begin flush with the left margin or be centred for emphasis.

10.18 Body of the letter

The body of the letter contains the message. Here, more than anywhere else, the general principle of communication applies: say it clearly yet succinctly, so that the reader will understand the message properly and quickly. Letters are normally single-spaced, with one blank line left between paragraphs. If a letter is very short, it may be double-spaced. When double spacing is used, the first line of each paragraph must be indented. Avoid writing paragraphs of more than ten lines. By the same token, do not divide a letter into many very short paragraphs.

10.19 Complimentary close

The complimentary close consists of such expressions as *Yours truly* or *Yours sincerely*. It is followed by a comma.

10.20   Signature

The handwritten or stamped signature comes first, followed by the title of the sender and of the organization. If someone else signs for the nominal sender, the order is as shown below:

> J. Doe
> for F. Buck
>> Chief, Publication Division

> **or**

> F. Buck
> Chief, Publication Division
> per J. Doe

10.21   Reference initials

The initials of the sender and of the transcriber are separated by a colon or oblique. The initials may be all in capital letters, all in small letters, or, most commonly, as follows:

> AB:cd

The information is not always needed but may be useful at a later time.

10.22   Enclosure notation

The notations *Enclosure(s)*, *Encl.*, *Attachment(s)* and *Att.* indicate that the envelope contains one or more documents in addition to the letter or attached to the letter. The number of such documents, if there are more than one, should appear after the notation.

10.23   Carbon copy notation

The indication *c.c.:* is followed by the names of the recipients of copies of the letter. It corresponds to the distribution list of documents such as memorandums and minutes, and lets the recipient know who else is receiving the message.

10.24   Postscript

A postscript is useful if the writer wishes to emphasize some point in the letter or, after the letter has been written, a point arises that should be included. The use of a postscript obviates the need to rewrite the letter. However, if the postscript sheds a completely new light on the message conveyed, the letter should probably be rewritten. Similarly, a postscript should not be used to attempt to compensate for a poorly organized letter. The notation *ps:* should be typed before the first word of the postscript and be indented if that is the letter format used. The postscript should begin on the second line below a carbon copy notation.

10.25   Model letter

Secrétariat   Secretary
d'État   of State

Our reference
3681-11

November 18, 1986

Your reference
675-21

Gail Carney
Co-ordinator
Official Languages Training Branch
Department of Supply and Services
Ottawa, Ontario
K1A 0S5

Dear Ms. Carney:

Thank you for your letter of November 13 concerning the possibility of some of your trainees working for our branch this summer.

It may be possible to arrange a four- to six-week on-the-job training period for your people in our units located in the National Capital Region. Naturally, you would have to assume all transportation costs and living expenses associated with such an arrangement. Please note also that trainees are expected to work in both official languages.

Enclosed is a questionnaire, which the trainees should fill out, have signed by their superior and then return to us.

Many thanks for your interest in our programs.

Yours sincerely,

Helen Van Uys
Director General
Linguistic Services Branch
Department of the Secretary of State
Ottawa, Ontario
K1A 0M5

Encl.

c.c.: C. Dupont

HVU/ld

Canada

Memorandums

10.26   Format

A memorandum is a short letter, note or report. The form most often used for memorandums within the federal public service is illustrated in the example (10.27).[2]

In the upper left part of the form appear the indications *To, From* and *Subject*. On the right are given the security classification (where applicable), the sender's and receiver's file references, if any, and the date.

If required, an indication of any attachments and a distribution list (*Distribution* or *c.c.:*) appear at the end of the document. This list can make communication more efficient because it tells the recipient who else is receiving the document.

See Chapter 11 for other suggestions.

---

2. CGSB Standard Form 22e [7540-21-865-6699]. This bilingual form allows the sender to communicate a short message in either French or English, usually to a person within the same department.

10.27   Model memorandum

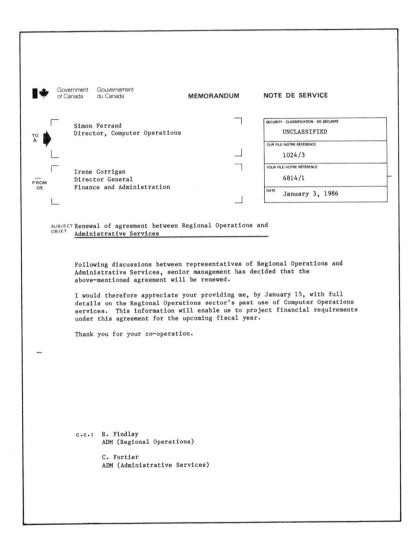

Government   Gouvernement
of Canada   du Canada   **MEMORANDUM**   **NOTE DE SERVICE**

TO
À   Simon Ferrand
           Director, Computer Operations

SECURITY · CLASSIFICATION · DE SÉCURITÉ	
UNCLASSIFIED	
OUR FILE/NOTRE RÉFÉRENCE	
1024/3	

FROM
DE   Irene Corrigan
           Director General
           Finance and Administration

YOUR FILE/VOTRE RÉFÉRENCE	
6814/1	
DATE	January 3, 1986

SUBJECT   Renewal of agreement between Regional Operations and
OBJET   Administrative Services

Following discussions between representatives of Regional Operations and
Administrative Services, senior management has decided that the
above-mentioned agreement will be renewed.

I would therefore appreciate your providing me, by January 15, with full
details on the Regional Operations sector's past use of Computer Operations
services. This information will enable us to project financial requirements
under this agreement for the upcoming fiscal year.

Thank you for your co-operation.

c.c.: R. Findlay
       ADM (Regional Operations)

       C. Fortier
       ADM (Administrative Services)

Eleven

Reports
and minutes

Reports

Minutes

11

Reports and minutes

Reports

11.01 Introduction

Almost everyone is called upon at some time to give a report, either oral or written, to a person or group. Minutes of meetings (see sections 11.19–11.24), the proceedings of conferences, seminars or colloquiums, and descriptions or reviews of books, concerts or motion pictures—these are all reports. Since a report is a communication, the same principle applies to it as to all communications: say or write it clearly and succinctly. In the case of a written report, the reader should be able to determine quickly who wrote it, for whom it was written, and why it was written.

11.02 Preparation

Before beginning to write a report, or even to collect data for it, determine who is expected to read the report and what use the reader is likely to make of it. The content and format of a report will be significantly affected by whether it is written for specialists or non-specialists, and whether it is an internal document for a limited number of persons or a report that may be distributed to members of the public. The purpose for which it is required is equally significant: it may be intended to note certain facts for information purposes, to make recommendations for action, to serve as a basis for discussion or debate, or to record the findings of an investigation or study.

Next, collect the data: documents, evidence, statistics and other possibly useful information. Then organize, analyse and evaluate the data collected, selecting what is essential. Finally, draw up a plan in chronological order, order of importance, or a combination of the two. Now you should be ready to write the report.

11.03 Format

A report may consist of a single paragraph or several volumes. A short report can be put on a memo sheet; a long report may be published. In either case the format should be appropriate to the nature and length of the report.

The long report will have a plan and consist of three parts: the introductory or preliminary matter; the body of the report; and the supplementary or back matter (see 11.09).

11.04 Preliminary matter

The preliminary matter contains, as needed, one or more of the following: the title of the report; the reason or reasons for writing the report; the authority for the investigation or study giving rise to the report; a preface, usually written by someone other than the author; acknowledgment of assistance or encouragement given to the author of the report; a table of contents; a list of tables; a list of figures; and, particularly in the case of a technical or scientific report, an abstract.

11.05 Title

A written report normally has a title. This title should accurately, clearly and concisely convey to the reader the subject of the report. The omission of verbs and articles, as is done in newspaper headlines, can condense the message. A title in two parts—the main title followed by a colon and subtitle—can make a long title seem shorter. The title must nevertheless contain all the key words needed for a proper description of the text.

11.06 Table of contents

In a long, complex report, a table of contents will be needed. The table should be accurate and detailed enough to tell the reader what each section is about. It will list all the main divisions of the report from the introduction to the appendixes. It will include accurate titles for the different parts and chapters, and give the main chapter divisions. The numbering system should be easy to follow.

11.07 Abstract or summary

A report that is to be published or to be presented as a university thesis will usually have an abstract, which will appear after the table of contents. It should be no more than 150–200 words long and be suitable for reprinting in a journal or collection of abstracts. An abstract is considered part of the preliminary matter. A summary, if needed, may run to several pages and is considered part of the body of the report. It may appear at the very beginning of the report proper or serve as a closing section at the end. Some reports may contain both an abstract and a summary.

The abstract or summary is prepared after the report is written and often by someone other than the author. It briefly indicates the purpose of the report, the method followed and observations made and, sometimes, the conclusions and recommendations. Its purpose is to enable a prospective reader to determine quickly whether the report contains information useful to her or him.

11.08 Body

The body or main text of the report describes for the reader the purpose, method and other circumstances of the activity being reported on (the introduction); the conduct of the experiment or other activity (the report proper); and the results, recommendations and comments (the conclusion).

The report proper develops the theme, giving details of the methods used and the observations or findings, and commenting on their significance. The body of the report ends with the results, conclusions and recommendations, if any.

The ideas should follow logically and smoothly from beginning to end. Any material that is not essential and might interfere with the flow of ideas should be put in a footnote or appendix, with a reference number referring to it at an appropriate place in the text. A footnote should not extend over more than one page. If it is too long to fit on one page, it belongs in an appendix. See Chapter 9 for detailed information on how to present footnotes.

A report that is the culmination of a study will probably contain footnotes and a bibliography. A serious yet common failing of writers of reports is inaccuracy, especially in quotations and references. If a quotation is not exact or is attributed to the wrong author, or if the date, volume number or page number of the reference is wrong, a reader who needs to refer to the source will waste time and lose patience. It is therefore wise to check all references both before and after they are inserted into the report.

11.09   Supplementary or back matter

After the body of the report comes the back matter, consisting of such elements as appendixes, references and a bibliography, and, if the report is long enough to require it, an index. The appendixes will contain notes and supplementary information such as copies of documents, formulas, statistical data, maps, charts, plans or drawings that the author believes will be useful to the reader.

11.10   Bibliography

A bibliography lists the works most often consulted for the report and works thought likely to be especially useful to the reader, even if not referred to in the text. See Chapter 9 for detailed information on the various ways of listing bibliographical entries.

11.11   Illustrations, tables and graphs

A well-prepared illustration such as a graph, picture or table can take the place of several paragraphs or even pages of narration, and thus help the author make, explain or emphasize a point strongly and succinctly.

Although illustrations can be grouped together in an appendix, the best place for them is in the text, as close as possible to the first mention of each illustration.

If two or three short pieces of statistical information are being conveyed, they can be incorporated into a sentence in the text. Otherwise it is better to show them in the form of a table. Furthermore, a chart, graph or diagram can reveal a trend or relationship that the reader might well have missed, even in a table.

The following rule applies to both graphs and photographs: fill the frame, but do not clutter it; include only what is essential.

11.12   Headings

Headings (or heads) are used to introduce a change of subject in a report or other document and to indicate subordination of topics. They are designed to guide the reader and enable him or her to find the pages where a particular topic is discussed. A heading's size and appearance should match its importance, and the same type of heading should be used consistently throughout a document to indicate subdivisions of the same degree of subordination.

The heading can be set off by various means depending, among other things, on the number of grades of heading and whether the document is to be printed or typed. These means include capitalization (full or initial letter or word only), underlining, centring, spacing, type size and the use of italic or boldface type. The specific means chosen to indicate the gradation of headings matter less than consistency in using them, and the system adopted should be as simple as the nature of the text will allow.

If there are many headings or subheadings of equal value, a numbering system, as used in this manual, can help to distinguish among them for reference purposes. Letters can be used for further subdivision of topics. This is less confusing than a system using several levels of numbers and producing subdivisions such as 1.4.2.3.

Punctuation should be kept to a minimum in headings, and their wording should be as succinct as possible without being ambiguous. No periods are required, except in run-in heads (see 9.14 for examples). Unless a heading is centred or full capitalization is used, only the first word and proper nouns are normally capitalized.

11.13   Margins

Make the top margin about 5 cm deep on the first page, so that the beginning is clearly marked, and 2.5 cm deep on the following pages. The bottom margin should be from 2.5 to 4 cm deep. The side margins should be at least 3 cm wide if room has to be allowed for stapling or binding; otherwise they can be narrower, but should be at least 1 cm wide in any case, to allow for possible reproduction on a duplicating machine and so that the complete text on both pages can be seen when the document is opened flat.

11.14   Spacing

There are two important requirements here. First, determine the minimum amount of space needed for clear separation of paragraphs, headings, extracts and illustrations. Second, be consistent in the spacing.

11.15   Pagination

The preliminary matter is numbered with Arabic or Roman numerals. The pages of the body of the text, beginning with the introduction, are numbered with Arabic numerals in the upper centre or upper right corner of the page.

11.16 Underlining

Underline book titles in the text, in footnotes and in bibliographies, or italicize them if this is a possibility (see 6.05).

Do not underline a heading in which all letters are capitalized.

11.17 Mathematics in reports

Keep in mind that equations $(a=b)$ and inequalities $(a \gtrless b)$ correspond to sentences in ordinary narrative and must therefore be grammatically correct. The expression $a=b$ is read "(The quantity) a is equal to (the quantity) b." The expression $a>b$ is read "(The quantity) a is greater than (the quantity) b."

When you write $E=mc^2$ you are writing an equation that is read "The amount of energy in a mass is equal to that mass multiplied by the square of the velocity of light." A formula, on the other hand, corresponds to a phrase and thus contains no equivalent of a verb. The formula for calculating E (the amount of energy in a given mass) is mc^2 (the mass multiplied by the square of the velocity of light).

Another principle to keep in mind is that equations and formulas can be written in more than one form. This is useful for fitting them on a page. For example, $\frac{a}{b}$ can be shown as a/b and thus take up only one line.

To eliminate a root sign, use an exponent, e.g. 6^{-2} in place of $\sqrt{6}$.

11.18 Other comments

The writer of a report will produce a much clearer document more quickly by ignoring the taboo against the use of the first person and by addressing the reader directly. If you try to be impersonal you will be forced to use the passive voice too often.

Minutes

11.19 Introduction

The minutes of a meeting are a record of the circumstances of the meeting, including the names of the participants, the topics discussed and the decisions reached. The minutes should include all essential information in as concise a form as possible. Special attention should be paid to the wording of resolutions, motions and other decisions, particularly if there is a chance that there will be differences of opinion on what was resolved, moved or decided. If it is a formal meeting, all motions must be written out verbatim.

11.20 Agenda

If the agenda is short and few decisions are to be made, it can be incorporated into the minutes. If the agenda is long and many points are to be discussed and acted on, the agenda may be omitted and the style used by the Department of National Defence adopted: a column at the left for the point discussed, and a column at the right for the person or body responsible for carrying out any action decided on, with the points being numbered. Alternatively, the points can be numbered and given subject headings. The agenda may include the items listed below, in the following order:

- welcoming of new members and guests
- reading and adoption of the agenda
- reading and adoption of the minutes of the previous meeting
- business arising out of the minutes
- other old business
- reading of correspondence
- committee reports
- items of business to be dealt with (listed)
- new business
- adjournment

See 11.21 for a model agenda.

11.21 Model agenda

Regional Development Branch
Meeting of Branch Executive Committee
Friday, January 17, 1986
9:00 a.m., Room 214
Agenda

1. Approval of BEC minutes of January 3, 1986
2. Senior Management Committee—debriefing
3. Assistant Deputy Minister—debriefing
4. Disk space allocation
5. Other business

11.22 Writing of minutes

The minutes may include the items listed below, in the following order:

- nature of the meeting (especially whether regular or special), date, time and place (if pertinent);
- identification of the person chairing the meeting;
- if necessary, the names of participants and of the organizations represented, and of persons who should have attended but were absent;
- identification of the person taking the minutes;
- the agenda, if short and if not distributed beforehand;
- body of the minutes, with the business being recorded in the order listed in the agenda; the names of persons responsible for taking action on the decisions reached may be given in a column at the right-hand margin;

· motion to adjourn or close the meeting;

· time of adjournment or closing of the meeting;

· signatures of the person who presided and of the person who took the notes;

· distribution list, if any.

11.23   Indirect speech

Note that, in minutes, indirect (reported) speech is generally required. Therefore the past and conditional forms of verbs should be used (e.g. *said*, not *says*; *had forecast*, not *has forecast*; *would decide*, not *will decide*).

See model memorandum for other examples. See 8.04 for more information on indirect speech.

11.24   Model minutes

Regional Development Branch
Minutes of Branch Executive Committee Meeting
Friday, January 17, 1986
9:00 a.m., Room 214

PRESENT:	R. Burnett (Chairperson)	M. Benesh
	B. Parkins	B. Boucher
	S. Garnett	A. Farrell (Secretary)

Action

1. Approval of BEC minutes of January 3, 1986

The minutes were approved with the following amendments:

Item 1—clarification
No decision had yet been made on what system   R. Burnett
would be used for person-year utilization as of
April 1, 1986. Mrs. Benesh requested that all
branch heads be advised in writing. This was
approved.

Item 2—clarification
The deadline could not be met because
decisions on some action items had yet to be
made.

2. SMC—debriefing

The Operational Planning Framework was dis-   B. Parkins cussed, but members did not get past the opening statement. It was agreed that the statement was incomplete and would be reviewed. A revised draft would be prepared.

3. ADM—debriefing

The Cabinet Agenda was discussed. Items covered included a paper on a water resources strategy for Canada, the Alberta Memorandum to Cabinet, the Dairy Program and the Livestock Pedigree Act.

The Deputy Minister and Mr. Burnett would be meeting with J. Faulds, the Regional Director for Nova Scotia, on January 21.

The Manitoba Memorandum of Understanding was signed on January 8.

4. Disk space allocation

The message from Colin Jamieson was sent to 35 out of 48 accounts in the Branch. Over 45 percent of our disk allocation was now in use. It was agreed that the Branch would not reduce its disk space allocation until the Branch Information Systems Committee met with Mr. Jamieson and obtained a clear definition of what the Branch required.

5. Other business—assignment

Alberta required a finance officer for a short-term assignment. Finance and Administration would be approached.   S. Garnett

The meeting closed at 10:00 a.m.

_____   _____

R. Burnett   A. Farrell

Distribution

ADM
Committee members

Twelve

Usages

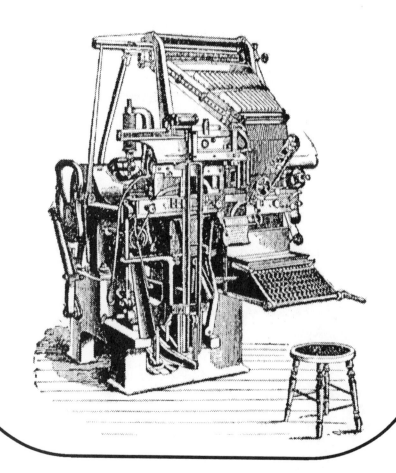

12

Usages

12.01 Introduction

The purpose of this chapter is to give the correct usage of many terms and expressions that are often misused because of inadequate knowledge of or sensitivity to proper idiom or because of confusion with a word having a similar sound or meaning.

12.02 Prepositional usage

The list below contains nouns, verbs, adjectives and adverbs which are often followed by the wrong preposition or, in some cases, are often followed by a preposition when, in fact, a different part of speech is required. The correct usage is given in each case.

abound in (A man abounding in natural ability.)

abound with (A faithful man shall abound with blessings.)

accord with

accord (of one's own)

account for

acquiesce in

adhere to

adverse to

agree on terms

agree to a proposal

agree to do (*not* accept to do)

agree with a person

aim at

alien to

associated with (*not* associated to)

averse to

aware of

begin by doing something

begin from a point

begin with an act

benefits of the benefactor

benefits to the beneficiary

capable of

capacity for

centre on (*not* around)

circumstances (in the)

compare with (*to note points of resemblance and difference*)

compare to (*only when used in the sense* to liken to)

concur in an opinion

concur with a person

conditions (under the)

conform to

conformity with (in)

consist in (*Definition:* Memory
consists in a present imagination
of past incidents.)

consist of (*Material:* The meal consisted of fish.)

consistent with

content oneself with

content others by doing

contrast (*When contrast is used as a verb, it is followed by*
with. *Either* to *or* with *may be used when the word*
contrast *is used as a noun.*)

conversant with

correspond to (resemble)

correspond with (communicate)

culminate in (*not* with)

demand for a thing

demand a thing from or of a person

derive from

differ, -ent, from (*preferred to* than, to)

differ with a person

disagree with a person

embark money in a business

embark on a ship, on a career

endowed with

forbid (one) to do

free from or of

immune from an obligation or something unpleasant

immune to a disease

indifferent to

infected with disease, bad qualities

infested with insects, wolves, vermin

initiative in (take the)

initiative (on one's own)

insensible to

insight into

invest in a business
invest with an office, a garment
join in a game
join with some person or thing
labour at a task
labour for a person, for an end
labour in a good cause
labour under a disadvantage
live by labour
live for riches
live on an income
look after a business
look at a thing
look for a missing article
look into a matter

look over an account
moment (on the spur of the)
moment's notice (at a)
oblivious of or to
parallel with or to
perpendicular to
point at a thing
point to a fact
possessed of wealth
possessed with an idea
prefer one to the other
prefer to do one thing rather than another
preference for
prevent from doing something
proceed against a person
proceed to an act not previously started
proceed with an act already started
prohibit from doing something
provide against ill luck
provide for an emergency
provide oneself with something
pursuant to (in pursuance of)
ready for a journey
ready to do something
ready with a reply
recommend that she do (*not* recommend her to do)
reference to (*preceded by* with, *not* in)

regard for a person (with regard to a subject)

regard for one's own interest

relief to suffering (bring)

relieve one of a duty

relieve with a tint

replace a person with another person (*but* a person is replaced by another)

responsibility (the) of deciding, of a position

responsibility for an action (assume)

responsible to a person for an action

result from an event

result in a failure

result (the) of an investigation

right of way, passage

right to do

satisfaction in an improvement (find)

satisfaction (the) of knowing

satisfaction to a person (give)

satisfied with a thing

secure against attack

secure from harm

secure in a position

substitute for

suggest that he do (*not* suggest him to do)

tamper with

unconscious of

variance on certain topics (at)

variance with a person (at)

versed in

view of the circumstances (in)

view to achieving a purpose (with a)

wary of a danger

12.03　Words commonly misused or confused

accept, except

Accept means "receive" or "say yes to"; *except* means "exclude" or "exempt":

The Director accepted the invitation to join the committee.

Canada was excepted from the general terms and conditions.

As a preposition, *except* means "other than":

No one except the secretary has access to the safe.

accuracy, precision

Accuracy is a measure of how close a fact or value approaches the true value and the degree to which something is free of error. *Precision* is a measure of the fineness of a value. Thus 6.0201 is more precise than 6.02, but it may not be more accurate.

affect, effect

Affect, as a verb, usually means "influence":

> Budgetary constraints have seriously affected our grants and contributions program.

As a verb, *effect* means "bring about"; as a noun, it means "result":

> Her promotion effected a change in her treatment of her colleagues.

> The Supreme Court ruling will have a lasting effect on official language services.

all right, alright

All right is the correct form. *Alright* should never be used.

allusion, illusion, delusion

An *allusion* is an indirect reference; *illusion* applies to something appearing to be true or real, but actually not existing or being quite different from what it seems. *Delusion* applies to a false and often harmful belief about something that does not exist:

> His allusion to the previous administration was out of place. Danby's paintings create a striking illusion of reality.

> The delusion that imports are always of unimpeachable quality must be dispelled.

alternate(ly), alternative(ly)

Alternate means "by turns," "one following another," or "every other one"; *alternative* refers to one of two or more possible choices. The same applies to the adverbial forms.

amount, number

Use *number* with things that can be counted; use *amount* for something considered as a mass or total:

> A number of employees fell sick.

> A large amount of grain is handled at Thunder Bay.

See also *fewer, lesser, less* below.

anyone, everyone

Anyone (*everyone, no one, someone*) is the correct form when the meaning is "anybody," "everybody," etc. *Any one* (*every one, no one, some one*) is the correct form when things and not persons are meant, or when an adjective is required, not a pronoun:

> Anyone can apply.

> We cannot rely on any one unit to handle the entire program.

appraise, apprize, apprise

Appraise means "set a value on"; *apprize* means "appraise" or "esteem"; *apprise* means "make aware of."

apt, liable, likely

Apt means "having a tendency (to) because of the subject's character" or "fitting, suitable"; *liable* expresses legal responsibility and the probability that the subject will suffer something undesirable or the fact that the subject is exposed to such a possibility if certain events occur; *likely* simply means "probable":

> We are apt to believe what we want to believe.

> This student is apt for a career in journalism.

> The company is liable to pay compensation in the event of work accidents.

> Children are liable to measles.

> The departmental reorganization is likely to occur before June.

as far as

Remember that this construction must be completed with a finite verb:

> As far as education funding is concerned (goes), the Department is still reviewing its position.

assume, presume

The material following *assume* expresses a theory or even a hypothesis, whereas the words following *presume* express what the subject believes to be the case for want of proof to the contrary:

> For the sake of argument, let us assume that our person-years will decrease by 10%.

> I presume that our budget has been pared as a result of the cutbacks.

basis, terms

On the basis of, on a . . . basis, in terms of, concerning and *with respect (regard) to* are overworked phrases which can often be replaced by a more concise construction:

> **not**
>
> She made her recommendations on the basis of the UN report.
>
> **but**
>
> She based her recommendations on the UN report.
>
> **not**
>
> Reports are filed on a monthly basis.
>
> **but**
>
> Reports are filed monthly.
>
> **not**
>
> In terms of the number of copies distributed, the manual was widely used.
>
> **but**
>
> Many copies of the manual were distributed.
>
> **not**
>
> Concerning (With regard to, With respect to) the working groups, they will start their projects on July 15.
>
> **but**
>
> The working groups will start their projects on July 15.

begin, commence

Begin is preferable to *commence* except in legal usage.

being as

Use *since, because* or *inasmuch as* instead of this colloquial expression.

beside, besides

Beside is a preposition normally meaning "by the side of." *Besides* is an adverb meaning "moreover" or, occasionally, a preposition meaning "in addition to" or "except":

> The clerk sat beside the machine.
>
> That division does not have the financial resources to carry out the project. Besides, nobody there is competent enough to handle it.

both, and

The material following *and* should correspond syntactically to the material following *both:*

> **Both** *her* supervisor and *her* director were on the selection board.

> **not**

> Both her supervisor and director were on the selection board.

characteristic, distinctive, typical

Typical relates to the characteristics peculiar to the type, class, species or group to which a thing or person belongs. The *characteristic* quality of something is the one that distinguishes and identifies it. *Distinctive* denotes an individuality that sets something apart from its type or group:

> The speech was typical of that brand of left-wing politics.

> The Deputy Minister always had that characteristic flourish at the end of her memorandums.

> The unit has a distinctive approach to training and development.

common, mutual

Common means "belonging to many or to all." *Mutual* means "reciprocal":

> Misspelling is a common problem.
> The couple's trust and respect are mutual.

Avoid using *mutual* redundantly as in "Canada and Mexico entered into a mutual agreement."

compare, contrast

Use *compare* to bring out likenesses, similarities (used with the preposition *to*) and when examining two or more objects to find likenesses or differences (used with the preposition *with*). Use *contrast* to point out differences:

> One could compare the leaderless team to a ship without a rudder.

> She compared her work plan with that of her colleague and found that she had been relatively conservative in her work-load forecasts.

> In contrast to my plan, his was very optimistic.

comprise, constitute, compose

The word *comprise* means "consist of"; do not use the expression *is comprised of*. *Constitute* and *compose* mean "make up, account for, form":

> The opera comprises five acts.

> The population of Ontario constitutes over 35% of the population of Canada.

> Five small communities together compose the city of Kanata.

continual, continuous

While these words are often synonymous, a fine distinction is that *continual* implies a close recurrence in time, a rapid succession of events. *Continuous* implies no interruption of an action:

> The new chief's continual carping alienated all his subordinates after a few months.

> The continuous whirring sound forced some employees to leave their work stations.

defective, deficient

Defective is that which is wanting in quality; *deficient* is that which is wanting in quantity:

> Sixteen of the machines were found to be defective and were scrapped.

> There was a deficiency of iron in his blood.

definitive, definite

Definitive means "conclusive, final" or "authoritative," whereas *definite* means "clear, unambiguous" or "having fixed limits":

> His thesis is the definitive work on oceanography.
> You must give a definite answer.
> You must specify a definite number of person-years.

dependant, dependent

Dependant is the noun, *dependent* the adjective:

> A wage earner with dependants is fully entitled to this deduction.

> Many Third World countries are dependent on food aid.

deprecate, depreciate

Deprecate means "express disapproval of"; *depreciate* means "lower the value of" or "become lower in value":

> The committee deprecated the official's under-the-table payments.

> Our trucks depreciate $1000 a year.

figuratively, literally, virtually

These words are often wrongly used to convey the exact opposite of their real meaning. *Figuratively* means "not literally, not really"; *literally* means "really, actually"; *virtually* means "almost entirely, for all practical purposes." Thus the statement "He was literally bowled over" is nonsensical. In the sentence "The sinking of the *Titanic* was a virtual disaster," the adjective is gratuitous and even detracts from the magnitude of the disaster.

disinterested, uninterested

Disinterested means "unbiased," while *uninterested* means "not interested in":

> Legal Services were asked to give a disinterested opinion.

> The Director General was uninterested in the projects presented by her staff.

each

Each must be treated as a singular and therefore requires a singular verb:

> Each of you now realizes the consequences.

either . . . or, neither . . . nor

Or is used with *either*, *nor* with *neither*. The constructions *either . . . or* and *neither . . . nor* should be used to co-ordinate two words, phrases or clauses:

> Either Mary or Philip will win the competition.
> Neither DRIE nor EMR is involved in the project.
> I communicated with him neither by telephone nor by correspondence.
> Either they go or I go.

emigrate, immigrate

The former means "leave"; the latter means "enter":

> A large number of Italians emigrated after the Second World War.
> It is forecast that the number of persons immigrating to Canada will gradually decline.

equally

This word should not be followed by *as*:

> Her plan is equally good.

fact

Exercise caution in using phrases such as *as a matter of fact*, *in fact*, *the fact is* and *actually*. They are often just an artificial means of assuring the reader that the writer is dealing with facts rather than theories and hypotheses, and may therefore be omitted in the interest of conciseness.

factor

A *factor* is something that contributes to an effect. Many writers use the word wrongly as a synonym for *circumstance, component, consideration, constituent, element, event* or *fact.*

fewer, lesser, less

Fewer is used when referring to number; *lesser* and *less* are used for quantity, amount or size:

> We will obtain fewer person-years than we did last year.
> The lesser of two evils.
> You will be assigned less work this week.

flaunt, flout

Flaunt means "display boastfully" but is often misused with the sense of "treat with contempt or scorn," a meaning properly assigned to *flout:*

> He insisted on flaunting his expertise.
> Employees should not flout the rules.

flounder, founder

Flounder means "struggle awkwardly without making progress." *Founder*, as a metaphor, means "fail":

> The program was floundering and clearly needed strong direction.
>
> The project foundered owing to lack of funds.

forecast

The preferred form of the past tense and past participle is *forecast*, not *forecasted.*

former, latter

Former and *latter* refer to only two units. For a group of more than two items, use *first* and *last* to indicate order.

fort, forte

Fort means "enclosed place" or "fortified building." *Forte* means "special accomplishment or ability":

> Last week we visited Fort Wellington.
> Languages are my forte.

healthful, healthy

Healthful means "conducive to health"; *healthy* means "possessing health":

> Healthy people have a healthful diet.

hung

The proper form when referring to capital punishment is *hanged.*

ideal

Ideal is an absolute. Do not write *more ideal*.

i.e., e.g., etc.

i.e. means "that is" and introduces a definition; *e.g.* means "for example." Do not use *e.g.* (or *for example* or a synonym such as *including*) and *etc.* in the same sentence, since *etc.* would be redundant:

not

The Minister received the representatives of many African countries, *e.g.* Angola, Mali, Tanzania, Zaire, Zimbabwe, *etc.*

but

The Minister received the representatives of many African countries, *e.g.* Angola, Mali, Tanzania, Zaire *and* Zimbabwe.

imply, infer

Imply refers to meaning intended by the speaker, while *infer* refers to meaning understood by the receiver of a message:

What did the official imply by that statement?
What should we infer from her statement?

include, comprise

Include implies only part of a whole; *comprise* implies all:

The multilateral working group includes two East Bloc representatives.

Water comprises hydrogen and oxygen.

in regards to

Omit the *s* at the end of *regard*.

inside of, off of, outside of

The *of* in each of these expressions is superfluous.

intense, intensive

Intense means "existing in a high degree, strong, extreme"; *intensive* means "deep and thorough":

He experienced intense pain.
Intensive study of the problem should yield results.

irregardless, disregardless

Both forms are incorrect. The correct word is *regardless*.

its, it's, its'

Its is the possessive form of it. *It's* is a contraction of *it is*. *Its'* is an incorrect form:

The committee amended its terms of reference.
It's an inappropriate term.

lead, led

Lead is the present tense of the verb *to lead*. *Led* is the past tense of the same verb and is often misspelled with *ea*:

Lead the way, captain!
Davis led from start to finish to win the gold medal.

least, less

It is incorrect to use *least* when comparing only two persons or things:

He is the less effective of the two programmers.

legible, readable

These terms can both mean "capable of being deciphered or read with ease." *Readable* also means "interesting to read":

The candidate's examination paper was barely legible.
I found Richler's latest book very readable.

luxuriant, luxurious

Luxuriant refers to abundant growth; *luxurious* concerns luxury:

The camp was surrounded by luxuriant vegetation.
The president's room was full of luxurious furniture.

media, medium

In the context of modern communications, *media* is the plural of *medium*. Use the singular when only one agency or means is referred to.

militate, mitigate

Militate means "act, work, operate (in favour of or against)"; *mitigate* means "reduce the severity of":

All these facts militate against renewal of the contract.
The government's policies are designed to mitigate the effects of unemployment.

more or less

Consider using *almost, approximately* or *virtually* instead of this overworked expression.

namely, etc.

Use introductory words like *namely, that is* and *for example* as little as possible. Very often they can be omitted altogether:

Three provinces were represented—(namely) British Columbia, Alberta and Saskatchewan.

need, needs

Both *needs* and *need* are used as the third person singular of the verb *need*, but in different contexts. *Needs* is the usual form in affirmative statements, either with noun objects or with *to* and an infinitive. *Need* is sometimes used, with an infinitive but without *to*, in negative statements and in questions. In formal English *need* may be used even when the negation is merely suggested by a word like *only*:

> She needs more management experience.
> He needs to practise.
> The director need not be informed.
> Need the director come?
> The department need only identify itself in the letterhead.

non
Avoid using this prefix to create new words when a suitable opposite already exists:

> inaudible **not** nonaudible
> disagreement **not** nonconcurrence

one of those who
Use a plural verb after *who*:

> She is one of those who always offer their assistance in a crisis.

on the part of
On the part of is often an awkward way of saying "by," "among," "for" or the like:

> A greater effort by (on the part of) your staff is required.

oral, verbal
Oral means "communicated by word of mouth"; *verbal* refers to a message communicated in words, whether spoken or written.

partially, partly
Partially can mean "incompletely" or "with partiality, in a biassed manner." *Partly* means "in part, to some extent." Use *partly* in the sense of "in part."

party, person, individual
Except with reference to telephone communications and in legal language, *party* refers to a group. *Individual* refers to a single person. As nouns, *individual* and *person* are synonymous. As an adjective, *individual* means "single" or "separate" and is therefore unnecessary and repetitious when used to modify *person* or when *each* has been used. In the phrases "individual person" and "each individual member," *individual* is redundant.

practicable, practical
Practicable means "that which can be done, which is feasible"; *practical* means "having to do with action or practice, fit for actual practice," and is the opposite of "theoretical."

reason is because
This phrase is incorrect. In standard English, a sentence beginning "The reason . . . is (was)" should be followed by a noun or a noun clause usually introduced by *that*:

> The reason why the trip was cancelled was lack of funds.

> The reason for the failure of the project was that the financial requirements had been underestimated.

refer, refer back
The word *back* is superfluous:

> Refer to the note on p. 1.

requisition
As a verb it is transitive and should not be followed by *for*:

> The clerk requisitioned supplies.

> **or**

> The clerk made a requisition for supplies.

> **not**

> The clerk requisitioned for supplies.

reserve, reservation
"Indian reserve" in Canada; "Indian reservation" in the United States.

responsible
Use *responsible* only with persons or corporate entities, not with things:

> The company was not responsible for the explosion.
> The supervisors must assume responsibility for their units' performance.

> **but**

> A gas leak caused the explosion.

sensual, sensuous
Sensuous means "pertaining to the senses, sensitive to beauty." *Sensual* means "pertaining to the satisfaction of physical desires, lewd, pertaining to the body":

> A sensuous appreciation of Ontario's wilderness is evident in the work of the Group of Seven.

> Is modern advertising to blame for our preoccupation with sensual pleasures?

statue, stature, statute

A *statue* is a sculpture. *Stature* can mean "status" and "prestige" or "height." A *statute* is a law:

> Champlain's statue is in that park.
> She is a historian of great stature.
> He is a man of tall stature.
> This statute has been amended.

these kind, those kind, these sort, those sort

Kind and *sort* are singular; *these* and *those* are plural. Write *this (that) kind, these (those) kinds, this (that) sort* and *these (those) sorts.*

thusly

Avoid this word; use *thus.*

till, until

Till and *until* are interchangeable as prepositions and as conjunctions. Avoid *'til* and *up until.*

try and, try to

The correct idiom is *try to.*

unique

This is an absolute. Do not write "very unique" or "rather unique." *Necessary, essential, perfect, empty, wrong, right, round, square* and many other adjectives are also absolute and should not be modified by a comparative adverb.

up

In many phrases *up* adds nothing to the meaning of the preceding verb; *up* is colloquial and wordy in such expressions as *choose up, finish up, listen up* and *wait up.*

where ... at

This phrase (as in *Where are we at?*) is colloquial and should not be used in writing.

who, whom

The former is the subject of a verb, the latter the object:

> Who will be selected?
> Whom will she hire?
> Tell me who was selected.
> Tell me whom she hired.

who's, whose

The form *who's* is a contraction of *who is. Whose* is the possessive form of *who.*

Appendixes

Appendix I

Appendix II

Appendix III

Appendix I

Geographical names

I.i Introduction

In a bilingual country like Canada, questions arise with particular acuteness on the designations to be used in official documents for cities, towns and villages, lakes, rivers and mountains, and other geographical entities and features which may have different but well-established designations in the two official languages or may be known by one name in one region and by a different one elsewhere.

In 1961 the federal government established the Canadian Permanent Committee on Geographical Names within the Department of Energy, Mines and Resources and assigned it the task of examining the problem and devising solutions to provide guidance for cartographers and writers of government documents. A policy for the treatment of geographical names on federal government maps and in written documents has now been formulated by this committee. It is stated below. First, however, it may be useful to review some of the issues that arise in Canadian toponymy, with particular reference to the translation of place names.

I.ii Generic and specific toponyms

A basic distinction in toponymy is that between a **generic** and a **specific** term. **Generic** terms include such designations as *lake, river, pond, city, street* and *mountain*, which describe the nature of the entity in question. A **specific** term, on the other hand, is the particular name applied to a geographical feature or location, e.g. *St. Lawrence* (River), *Rocky* (Mountains) or (Lake) *Louise*. It is generally agreed that it is permissible to translate generic terms, since they are not an integral part of the toponym.[1] The question whether to translate specific terms is more complicated and, as will be seen, lends itself to solution only on a case-by-case basis.

It raises, for example, the issue of how to treat the relatively large number of toponyms having specifics derived from common, descriptive nouns. Some of them, such as the *Rocky* Mountains and Lake *Superior*, have well-established versions in both official languages, but others (*Round* Lake, Lac *Noir*, *Beaver* Lake, Cap à l'*Orignal*, etc.) may be known by only a single designation existing in the language of the locality. Is majority local usage to be the criterion of correctness, or should two official versions of such toponyms be allowed?

---

1. See Jean-Yves Dugas, "Terminologie et toponymie: un mariage de raison," *L'Actualité Terminologique / Terminology Update* (March 1982): 1–6; L. Fillion, "Pour une politique fédérale du traitement linguistique des noms géographiques," *L'Actualité Terminologique / Terminology Update* (Aug.–Sept. 1982): 1–6.

I.iii Policy

The solution devised by the Canadian Permanent Committee on Geographical Names is twofold. First, regarding maps, the policy is to write geographical names as they are spelled in their official form—"official" meaning the form found in the *Gazetteer of Canada* and the *Répertoire toponymique du Québec*. Thus *Québec* (the city), *Montréal, Trois-Rivières, St John's, Lac Saint-Jean* and *Madawaska River* are the official forms on both French and English maps. The only exceptions to this rule are some eighty names of "Pan-Canadian significance" (see list below) where the generic—and often the specific—is translated. Since *Quebec* (the province) is among these names, it is to be written in English without the accent, whereas *Québec* (the city) retains the accent.

Second, as it applies to written documents, the policy on populated places is the same as that for maps. With respect to physical features, it is stipulated that the generic, but never the specific, is translated. Thus *Lac Saint-Jean* becomes *Lake Saint-Jean* in an English text (note retention of the hyphen). Again, the eighty-odd names of Pan-Canadian significance constitute an exception: *Georgian Bay*, for example, will appear in French texts as *Baie Georgienne*, with both the generic and the specific translated.

For more precise information on the background and application of this policy, the reader is referred to Treasury Board Circular No. 1983-58 of November 23, 1983.

I.iv List of names of Pan-Canadian significance

The following is the complete list of names of Pan-Canadian significance drawn up by the Canadian Permanent Committee on Geographical Names:

Abitibi, Lake / Lac Abitibi
Anticosti Island / Île d'Anticosti
Appalachian Mountains / Les Appalaches
Arctic Ocean / Océan Arctique
Athabasca, Lake / Lac Athabasca
Athabasca River / Rivière Athabasca
Atlantic Ocean / Océan Atlantique

Baffin Bay / Baie de Baffin
Baffin Island / Île de Baffin
Beaufort Sea / Mer de Beaufort
Belle Isle, Strait of / Détroit de Belle-Isle
British Columbia / Colombie-Britannique

Cabot Strait / Détroit de Cabot
Cape Breton Island / Île du Cap-Breton
Chaleur Bay / Baie des Chaleurs
Champlain, Lake / Lac Champlain
Churchill River, Man. / Rivière Churchill (Man.)
Churchill River, Nfld. / Fleuve Churchill (T.-N.)
Coast Mountains / Chaîne Côtière
Columbia River / Fleuve Columbia

Davis Strait / Détroit de Davis

Ellesmere Island / Île d'Ellesmere
Erie, Lake / Lac Érié

Franklin, District of / District de Franklin
Fraser River / Fleuve Fraser
Fundy, Bay of / Baie de Fundy

Georgian Bay / Baie Georgienne
Great Bear Lake / Grand lac de l'Ours
Great Slave Lake / Grand lac des Esclaves

Hudson Bay / Baie d'Hudson
Hudson Strait / Détroit d'Hudson
Huron, Lake / Lac Huron

James Bay / Baie James

Keewatin, District of / District de Keewatin

Labrador Sea / Mer du Labrador
Laurentian Mountains / Les Laurentides

Mackenzie, District of / District de Mackenzie
Mackenzie River / Fleuve Mackenzie
Manitoba, Lake / Lac Manitoba
Michigan, Lake / Lac Michigan (not actually in Canada)

Nelson River / Fleuve Nelson
New Brunswick / Nouveau-Brunswick
Newfoundland / Terre-Neuve
Niagara Falls / Chutes Niagara
Nipigon, Lake / Lac Nipigon

Nipissing, Lake / Lac Nipissing
North Saskatchewan River / Rivière Saskatchewan Nord
Northumberland Strait / Détroit de Northumberland
Northwest Territories / Territoires du Nord-Ouest
Nova Scotia / Nouvelle-Écosse

Ontario, Lake / Lac Ontario
Ottawa River / Rivière des Outaouais

Pacific Ocean / Océan Pacifique
Peace River / Rivière de la Paix
Prince Edward Island / Île-du-Prince-Édouard

Quebec / Québec (province)
Queen Charlotte Islands / Îles de la Reine-Charlotte
Queen Elizabeth Islands / Îles de la Reine-Élisabeth

Rainy Lake / Lac à la Pluie
Rainy River / Rivière à la Pluie
Red River / Rivière Rouge
Restigouche River / Rivière Restigouche
Rocky Mountains / Montagnes Rocheuses

Sable Island / Île de Sable
Saguenay River / Rivière Saguenay
St. Clair, Lake / Lac Sainte-Claire
Saint John River / Rivière Saint-Jean
St. Lawrence, Gulf of / Golfe du Saint-Laurent
St. Lawrence River / Fleuve Saint-Laurent
Saskatchewan River / Rivière Saskatchewan
South Saskatchewan River / Rivière Saskatchewan Sud
Superior, Lake / Lac Supérieur

Timiskaming, Lake / Lac Témiscamingue

Ungava Bay / Baie d'Ungava

Vancouver Island / Île de Vancouver

Winnipeg, Lake / Lac Winnipeg
Winnipegosis, Lake / Lac Winnipegosis
Winnipeg River / Rivière Winnipeg
Woods, Lake of the / Lac des Bois

Yukon River / Fleuve Yukon
Yukon Territory / Territoire du Yukon

Appendix II

Elimination of
Sexual, Racial and Ethnic Stereotyping
in Written Communications

II.i Introduction

A Government of Canada document entitled "Elimination of sexual stereotyping"[1] defines sexual stereotyping as "the use of words, actions, and graphic material that assigns roles or characteristics to people solely on the basis of sex, and without regard for the intrinsic potentials of women and men" and goes on to state that it is the policy of the Government to eliminate sexual stereotyping from all government communications.

On the basis that communications have a cumulative impact on people's perceptions, behaviour and aspirations, that most communications reach an audience composed equally of women and men, and that women are the prime targets of sexual stereotyping, the document then presents a number of guidelines for written material.

In February 1984 the Government of Canada issued "Guidelines for the Representative Depiction of Visible and Ethnic Minorities and Aboriginal Peoples in Government Communications."[2] The Guidelines are based on the principle that all groups, irrespective of ancestry and ethnic origin, are and must be portrayed as equally productive and contributing members of Canadian society. They are intended to help correct biases and stereotypes which constitute barriers to full participation in that society. In practical terms, they require that material "be reviewed for words, images and situations that reinforce erroneous preconceptions or suggest that all or most members of a racial or ethnic group are the same."

This appendix lists many of the stereotyping problems covered in the two federal government documents and in other pertinent material, and shows how those problems can be solved. The objective in the case of both women and minority groups is to ensure equal treatment in writing, to depict them as fully participating members of society, and to eliminate preconceived ideas about their functions and attributes.

Elimination of Sexual Stereotyping

II.ii Correspondence; names and forms of address

The form preferred or used by the person being addressed or referred to should be retained if it is known. Otherwise, the following guidelines should be applied in order to ensure uniform and equal treatment of the sexes.

---

1. Treasury Board, *Administrative Policy Manual*, Chapter 484.

2. Treasury Board, Circular No. 1984-4.

- If the sex of the addressee is not known, begin your reply with "Dear" followed by the initials and the surname:

  Dear J. D. Simmonds:

Where neither sex nor name is known, use the form "Dear Sir/Madam."

- When the names of a woman and man are mentioned together, use parallel language so that women are portrayed as equals, not appendages:

  Alan Knight and Joyce Philips

  J. Philips and A. Knight

  Knight and Philips

  Joyce Philips, the engineer, and Alan Knight, the journalist

  not

  Alan Knight and Mrs. J. Philips

  or

  Alan Knight, the journalist, and Mrs. J. Philips

- Ensure parallel treatment of couples:

  Mr. and Mrs. James and Irene Luciano

  James and Irene

  Mr. and Mrs. Luciano

  James and Irene Luciano

  not

  Mr. and Mrs. James Luciano

  or

  James Luciano and his wife Irene

- Ensure parallel treatment of work associates:

  Raymond Kovacs and his assistant Karen White

  not

  Mr. Kovacs and his assistant Karen

- Alternate order of reference so that women are not always given second place:

  Karen White and her immediate superior, Raymond Kovacs

  Karen and Raymond

  Joyce Philips and Alan Knight

- In distribution and other lists, use alphabetical order or list according to rank.

II.iii   Pronouns

Because English lacks a singular pronoun that signifies the non-specific "he or she," customarily the masculine pronoun has been used. The following guidelines serve to avoid this usage.

• Eliminate the pronoun completely:

not

The section chief is responsible for maintaining good relations with clients. He ensures that deadlines are met.

but

The section chief is responsible for maintaining good relations with clients *and ensuring* that deadlines are met.

• Repeat the noun:

not

An employee must file a grievance within the prescribed time limit. *His* union representative will already be involved at this stage of the process.

but

An employee must file a grievance within the prescribed time limit. *The employee's* union representative will usually be involved at this stage of the process.

• Use the plural:

not

Each responsibility centre manager must prepare *his* own work plans.

but

All responsibility centre managers must prepare *their* own work plans.

• Use a neutral word such as "one," "individual" or "incumbent":

not

his duties

but

the incumbent's duties

• Use both pronouns:

her or his employees

his or her duties

• Alternate the use of the masculine and feminine forms throughout your text so that neither predominates.

II.iv   Personification

Avoid using the feminine pronoun to personify animals, events, ships, etc.:

not

Once again the area was hit by hurricane Flora. *She* wrought havoc.

but

... *It* wrought havoc.

II.v   Position titles and occupational terms

Eliminate titles and terms which suggest that a job is not typically performed by a woman (or man) or that the task, when performed by a woman, is not the same. As far as possible, job titles should not imply that the job can be filled only by members of one sex.

- Do not feminize titles by adding *ess*, as in "manageress", and do not add gratuitous modifiers, as in "*lady* doctor" or "*male* nurse."
- Use feminine nouns, when women are referred to, or sex-inclusive nouns, where men are not specifically referred to, provided that undue violence is not done to the language:

  spokeswoman/spokesperson   **not**   spokesman

  the French   **not**   Frenchmen

  councillor   **not**   councilman

  cleaner   **not**   cleaning woman

II.vi   Man, lady, girl, woman

- Avoid, where possible, the generic *man* as part of a compound:

  anybody, anyone   **not**   a man

  nobody, no one   **not**   no man

  labour force, work force, personnel, staff   **not**   manpower

  writer   **not**   man of letters

  artificial   **not**   man-made

  humanity, people   **not**   mankind

  ordinary people   **not**   the man in the street

- Unless a minor is referred to or you wish to evoke refinement or high standing, do not use *girl* or *lady*, use *woman*:

> The men and women of the Administrative Support Division

> **not**

> The men and girls of the Administrative Support Division

> Seventy percent of the delegates were women.

> **not**

> Seventy percent of the delegates were ladies.

II.vii Full range of human characteristics and situations

Women should be treated with equal respect and dignity without gratuitous reference to physical characteristics, and depicted as living and working in a variety of circumstances and assuming a range of responsibilities without reference solely to their roles as wife, mother, etc. unless it is in this context that they are being mentioned.

- Avoid gratuitous reference to physical or other characteristies and undue emphasis on a woman's family role:

> Dr. and Mrs. Rolfe

> John and Dora Rolfe

> **not**

> Dr. Rolfe and his charming blonde wife Dora

> Publisher Henry Conti and his daughter Tanya Devonshire,
> a lawyer practising in Winnipeg

> **not**

> Publisher Henry Conti and his daughter Tanya

- Do not suggest that men are the norm in certain situations and women in others. Show that members of each sex are now performing roles that were traditionally the preserve of the other sex:

> Parent and child

> **not**

> Mother and child

> People (**or** Families) are suffering increasingly from the
> burden of taxation.

> **not**

> Men and their families are suffering increasingly from the
> burden of taxation.

Professionals, their spouses and their children

not

Professionals, their wives and their children

the average worker

or

the average wage-earner

not

the average working man

- Ensure that women as a group are treated with respect, particularly in the role of homemaker. Refer to "women re-entering the work force," not to "women going back to work." Do not refer to "working women" or "working wives" in contrast to homemakers; use the expression "women earning a wage" or an equivalent.

Elimination of
Racial and Ethnic Stereotyping

II.viii   Ethnic clichés

Eliminate and avoid expressions which cloud the fact that all attributes may be found in all groups: for example, "*inscrutable* Orientals," "*frugal* Scots" and "*amorous* Italians."

II.ix   Gratuitous modifiers

Avoid modifiers which reinforce racial and ethnic stereotypes by giving information that suggests an exception to the rule:

not

The board interviewed a number of intelligent Black students.

but

. . . a number of Black students.

or

. . . a number of intelligent students.

II.x   Connotative modifiers

Be cautious in using adjectives that, in certain contexts, have questionable racial or ethnic connotations or insulting, often racist overtones, such as *primitive, conniving, savage, lazy, backward, yellow, red* and *black.*

II.xi   Identification of groups

Be aware of the self-identification preferences of racial and cultural groups:

Inuk, Inuit **not** Eskimo

Black **not** Negro

Appendix III

Proofreader's Marks

III.i Introduction

It is essential to eliminate typographical, spelling, punctuation and other errors of form if you want a piece of writing to have its full effect—hence the importance of good proofreading.

Prepare copy by typing double-spaced with a 4 cm line space around all copy. Proofreading marks can be made on the right-hand space in red ink and editing notes can be made on the left-hand space in another colour.

III.ii Common proofreader's marks and their use

Style of type

w f //	Wrong front (size or style of type)
lc.	Set in LOWER CASE or LOWER CASE
≡ *caps*	SET IN capitals
c & sc	Set in Caps & Small Caps
lc. & u.c.	Lower Case with Initial Caps
sm caps	Set in small capitals
rom.	Set in roman (or regular) type
ital.	Set in italic (or oblique) type
l.f.	Set in lightface type
bf.	**Set in boldface type**
\7/	Set superior character[7]
/7\	Set inferior character[7]

Positioning

⌐	Move to right
⌐	Move to left
‖	Align vertically
tr.	Transpose letter in a word
tr.	Transpose enclosed in ring matter
⌐ ⌐	Set in centre
⌐ ⌐	Square off or full measure

Delete or insert

ℓ Delete, take out

stet Let it stand—(all ~~matter~~ above dots)

O.S.C. Out see copy
If possible, make photocopy and
staple to page with OSC marked.

Paragraphing

¶ Begin a paragraph

no ¶ No paragraph

run on Run on

flush ¶ No paragraph indention

Spacing

l/s LETTER SPACE

Insert space (or more space)

☐ En quad space or indention

☐ Em quad space or indention

☐ 2 quad space or indention

◡ Close up entirely; take out space

◡ Less space between words

eq # Equalize space between words

Punctuation

⊙   Insert a period ⅄

⊚   Insert a semicolon ⅄

⋏   Insert a comma ⅄

⊙   Insert a colon ⅄

⋏   Apostrophe or single quote ⅄

ᵛ⁄ ᵛ⁄   Quotation marks or quotes ⅄

?⁄   Question mark or "query" ⅄

!⁄   Exclamation mark ⅄

=⁄   Insert hyphen ⅄

|⊥ₘ| Insert EM dash ⅄

|⊥ₙ| Insert EN dash ⅄

(⁄)   Parentheses ⅄

[⁄]   Brackets ⅄

Miscellaneous

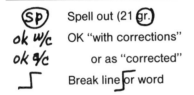

(SP)   Spell out (21 gr.)

ok w/c   OK "with corrections"

ok a/c   or as "corrected"

⌐   Break line or word

III.iii   **Example of proofread page**

2 line #

]Emphasis on back injury reduction [

1 line #

[During recent years work injury rates for the public   ⋀   *u.c.*

service of Canada have shown a consistent delcine. In   *e/*

1983/84, this trend towards improved health and safety

has been maintained, with the overall PS injury frequen-   ⓈⓅ

cy rate assessed at 4.5 injuries per 100 person years,   *=/*

representing an 8 per cent decrease over that of the   *t/*

previous year. Similarly, the severity injury rate also   **tr.**

decreased by 8 per cent, to 29.1 days lost per 100

person-years.

These injury and severity rates, compiled from work in-

jury reports submitted under the Government Employees'   *ital.*

Compensation Act, are the accepted performance in-

dicators (for) reporting and comparing work injury   **stet**

experience, for the fiscal year during which the work

injuries are incurred. In comparing the performances of   ⁋

individual departments during 1982/83 with the previous

year, 12 departments had fewer injuries 10 reported no   *tr./*   ⋀

injuries and the remainder experienced little or no   ⋀

change in their rates. This overall improvement in the   **stet**

work injury and severity rates suggest that the Public   *#/delete/s/*

Service Occupational Health and Safety Program is   ⋎

having a positive impact. A variety of new health and

safety program initiatives are under way or in the   *lc./ which/*

planing stage will, with the cooperation and participa-   *n/ =/*

tion of operating departments, help to maintain these

positive results See list attached   *!/ !/*

III.iv   Glossary of terms

Alterations	Changes made in the copy after it has been set in type.
Bullets	Series of dots.
Composition	General term for typesetting material.
Folio	The page number.
Font	The complete assortment of type of one size and face.
Italic	The style of letters that slope forward, in contrast to upright or roman letters.
Justify	To adjust spacing in a line so that all lines are equally long.
Leaders	Dots or dashes.
Letterspace	The space between letters—usually in display type, headlines, etc.
Measure	Width of line of type, always indicated in picas.
Pica	Unit of measure about 1/6 inch.
Point	There are 12 points to a pica.
Roman	A standard or upright typeface.
San-serif	A typeface without serifs.
Serif	The short cross-lines at the ends of the main strokes of many letters in some typefaces.
Small caps	An alphabet of small capital letters in the size of the lower-case letters.
Stet	A proofreader's mark signifying that copy marked should remain as it was.
Widow	A word or short line at the top of a page.
Wrong font	The mark "WF" indicates a letter or figure of the wrong size or face.

Selected Bibliography

I Dictionaries

Acronyms, Initialisms & Abbreviations Dictionary 1985–86. 3 vols. Edited by Ellen T. Crowley and Helen E. Sheppard. 9th ed. Detroit: Gale Research Co., 1984.

Authors' and Printers' Dictionary. Edited by F. Howard Collins. 11th rev. ed. London: Oxford University Press, 1973.

A Dictionary of Canadianisms on Historical Principles. Toronto: W. J. Gage Ltd., 1973.

The Gage Canadian Dictionary. Toronto: Gage Publishing Ltd., 1983.

The Random House Dictionary of the English Language. New York: Random House, 1981.

The Shorter Oxford English Dictionary on Historical Principles. 2 vols. 3rd ed. with rev. addenda. Oxford: Clarendon Press, 1980.

Webster's Ninth New Collegiate Dictionary. Markham, Ont.: Thomas Allen & Son Limited, 1983.

Webster's Third New International Dictionary of the English Language, Unabridged. Springfield, Mass.: G. & C. Merriam Co., 1981.

The Winston Dictionary of Canadian English. Toronto: Holt, Rinehart and Winston of Canada Ltd., 1975.

II Canadian and International Standards

Anglo-American Cataloguing Rules. 2nd ed. Edited by Michael Gorman and Paul W. Winckler. Ottawa: Canadian Library Association, 1978.

Canada. Department of Consumer and Corporate Affairs. Metric Commission Canada. *Metric Press Guide*. 2nd ed. Metric Commission Canada, n.d.

————— . Treasury Board. *Administrative Policy Manual*, Chapter 470, "Federal Identity Program." Ottawa, 1982.

————— . Treasury Board. Federal Identity Program. *Design Guide*. Ottawa, 1979.

————— . Treasury Board. Office of the Comptroller General of Canada. Circular No. 1979-7, "Writing Dollar Amounts on Payment Instruments and Other Documents." Ottawa, 1979.

————— . Treasury Board. Office of the Comptroller General. Circular No. 1984-64, "Standard for Writing Dollar Amounts on Payment Instruments and Certain Other Documents." Ottawa, 1984.

————— . Treasury Board. Circular No. 1983-58, "Official Languages and Geographical Names on Federal Government Maps." Ottawa, 1983.

Canadian Standards Association. *Canadian Metric Practice Guide*. Rexdale, Ont., 1979. (CAN3-Z234.1-79)

Canadian Standards Association. *Metric Editorial Handbook*. Rexdale, Ont., 1980. (CSA Special Publication Z372-1980)

International Organization for Standardization. International Standard ISO 4. *Documentation—International Code for the Abbreviation of Titles of Periodicals*. 1st ed. Geneva, 1972.

————— . International Standard ISO 31/0. *General Principles concerning Quantities, Units and Symbols*. 2nd ed. Geneva, 1981.

————— . International Standard ISO 690. *Documentation—Bibliographical References—Essential and Supplementary Elements*. 1st ed. Geneva, 1975.

————— . International Standard ISO 832. *Documentation—Bibliographical References—Abbreviations of Typical Words*. 1st ed. Geneva, 1975.

———— . International Standard ISO 999. *Documentation—Index of a Publication*. 1st ed. Geneva, 1975.

———— . International Standard ISO 2014. *Writing of Calendar Dates in All-Numeric Form*. 1st ed. Geneva, 1976.

———— . International Standard ISO 2384. *Documentation—Presentation of Translations*. 1st ed. Geneva, 1977.

———— . International Standard ISO 3307. *Information Interchange—Representations of Time of the Day*. 1st ed. Geneva, 1975.

III General Reference Works

Buttress, F. A. *World Guide to Abbreviations of Organizations*. 7th ed. London: Leonard Hill, 1984.

Canada. Department of Energy, Mines and Resources. Canadian Permanent Committee on Geographical Names. *Gazetteer of Canada*. 12 vols. Ottawa, 1966–84.

———— . Department of National Defence. *Manual of Abbreviations*, Ottawa, 1980. (A-AD-12 1-FOI/IX-000)

———— . Department of Supply and Services. *Organization of the Government of Canada 1980 L'administration fédérale du Canada 1980*. Ottawa, 1980.

Canada Year Book 1985. A Review of Economic, Social and Political Developments in Canada. Ottawa: Statistics Canada, 1985.

Canadian Almanac and Directory 1985. Edited by Susan Bracken. Toronto: Copp Clark Pitman, 1985.

Canadian Who's Who. Edited by Kieran Simpson. Toronto: University of Toronto Press, 1985.

Colombo, John Robert. *Colombo's Canadian References*. Toronto: Oxford University Press, 1976.

Colombo's Canadian Quotations. Edited by John Robert Colombo. Edmonton: Hurtig Publishers, 1974.

Directory of Associations in Canada / Répertoire des associations du Canada. Edited by Brian Land. 6th ed. Toronto: University of Toronto Press, 1985.

Encyclopedia Canadiana. 10 vols. Toronto: Grolier of Canada Ltd., 1977.

Lowe, D. Armstrong. *A Guide to International Recommendations on Names and Symbols for Quantities and on Units of Measurement*. Geneva: World Health Organization, 1975.

Measures, Howard. *Styles of Address. A Manual of Usage in Writing and in Speech*. 3rd ed. Toronto: Macmillan, 1974.

The Canadian Encyclopedia. 3 vols. Edited by James H. Marsh. Edmonton: Hurtig Publishers, 1985.

1985 Corpus Almanac & Canadian Sourcebook. 2 vols. 20th annual ed. Edited by C. E. Clarke. Don Mills, Ont.: Southam Communications Ltd., 1985.

1984 Canadian Trade Index. Toronto: Canadian Manufacturers' Association, 1984.

Québec. Commission de Toponymie. *Répertoire toponymique du Québec*. Québec: Éditeur officiel, 1981.

IV Manuals of Style and Usage

American Chemical Society. *Handbook for Authors*. Washington, D.C., 1978.

American Institute of Physics. *Editorial Handbook*. New York, 1976.

American Institute of Physics. *Style Manual*. 3rd rev. ed. New York, 1978.

American Medical Association. *Stylebook / Editorial Manual*. Littleton, Mass.: Publishing Sciences Group, Inc., 1976.

Baker, Sheridan. *The Practical Stylist*. New York: Harper & Row, 1985.

Ball, Alice Morton. *Compounding in the English Language*. New York: H. H. Wilson Co., 1939.

Bernstein, Theodore M. *The Careful Writer. A Modern Guide to English Usage*. New York: Atheneum, 1965.

Canada. *Civil Service of Canada Office Manual / Manuel de Bureau, Service civil du Canada*. Ottawa: Queen's Printer, 1964.

———— . Department of Energy, Mines and Resources. Geological Survey of Canada. *Guide to Authors*. Ottawa, 1980.

———— . Department of National Defence. *DND Administrative and Staff Procedures Manual: Administrative Procedures for NDHQ*. Ottawa, 1976.

———— . Office of the Auditor General. *A Writer's Handbook*. 2nd rev. ed. Ottawa, 1981.

The Canadian Press. *Canadian Press Stylebook: A Guide for Writers and Editors*. Toronto, 1983.

———— . *Caps and Spelling*. Toronto, 1981.

The Chicago Manual of Style. 13th ed. rev. and expanded. Chicago: University of Chicago Press, 1982.

Copperud, Roy H. *American Usage and Style: The Consensus*. New York: Van Nostrand Reinhold Co., 1980.

Corder, J. W., and W. S. Avis. *Handbook of Current English*. Toronto: Gage Publishing Ltd., 1983.

Council of Biology Editors. *Style Manual*. 4th ed. Arlington, Va., 1978.

Follett, Wilson. *North American Usage: A Guide*. Edited by Jacques Barzun et al. New York: Grosset & Dunlap, Inc., 1970.

Fowler, H. W. *A Dictionary of Modern English Usage*. 2nd ed. Revised by Sir Ernest Gowers. Oxford: Oxford University Press, 1965; rpt. 1983.

Fowler, H. W., and F. G. Fowler. *The King's English*. 3rd ed. London: Oxford University Press, 1931; rpt. 1974.

The Globe and Mail Style Book. Edited by E. C. Phelan. 5th ed. rev. and extended. Toronto, 1981.

Gowers, Sir Ernest. *The Complete Plain Words*. Harmondsworth: Penguin Books, 1973; rpt. 1979.

Mager, N. H., and S. K. Mager. *Encyclopedic Dictionary of English Usage*. Englewood Cliffs, N.J.: Prentice-Hall, Inc., 1974.

Mandel, Siegfried. *Writing for Science and Technology*. New York: Dell Publishing, 1970.

Messenger, William E., and Jan de Bruyn. *The Canadian Writer's Handbook*. Scarborough, Ont.: Prentice-Hall, 1980.

MLA Handbook for Writers of Research Papers. 2nd ed. New York: Modern Language Association, 1984.

Mullins, Carolyn J. *A Guide to Writing and Publishing in the Social and Behavioral Sciences*. New York: John Wiley and Sons, 1977; rpt. 1983.

The New York Times Manual of Style and Usage. Revised and edited by Lewis Jordan. New York: Times Books, 1982.

Partridge, Eric. *Usage and Abusage. A Guide to Good English*. New York: Greenwood Press, 1969.

———— . *You have A Point There*. London: Routledge & Kegan, 1978.

Perrin, Porter G. *Writer's Guide and Index to English*. 3rd ed. Chicago: Scott, Foresman and Co., 1959.

Sabin, William A. *A Reference Manual for Secretaries and Typists.* 2nd Canadian ed. Toronto: McGraw-Hill Ryerson Ltd., 1978.

Shaw, Harry. *Handbook of English.* Revised by Dave Carley. 4th Canadian Edition. Toronto: McGraw-Hill Ryerson, 1985.

Strunk, W., Jr., and E. B. White. *The Elements of Style.* 3rd ed. New York: Macmillan, 1979.

United States Government Printing Office. *Style Manual.* Rev. ed. Washington, D.C., 1984.

Van Hagan, Charles E. *Report Writers' Handbook.* Englewood Cliffs, N.J.: Prentice-Hall, Inc., 1969.

Wood, Frederick T. *Current English Usage: A Concise Dictionary.* London: Macmillan and Co., 1962.

V   Other Works on Language and Related Subjects

Dugas, Jean-Yves. "Terminologie et toponymie: un mariage de raison." *L'Actualité Terminologique / Terminology Update*, 15, 3 (March 1982): 1–6.

Fillion, Laurent. "Pour une politique fédérale du traitement linguistique des noms géographiques." *L'Actualité Terminologique / Terminology Update*, 15, 7 (Aug.–Sept. 1982): 1–6.

Kirby, Patricia. "English Word Division." *Termiglobe*, VII, 4 (Nov. 1984): 24–25.

Lauriston, Andy. "Hyphenation" (Part One). *Termiglobe*, VI, 4 (Nov. 1983): 22–23.

————. "Hyphenation" (Part Two). *Termiglobe*, VI, 5 (Jan. 1984): 29–30.

Orkin, Mark M. *Speaking Canadian English.* Toronto: General Publishing Co. Ltd., 1970.

Potter, Simeon. *Changing English.* 2nd rev. ed. London: André Deutsch, 1975.

Scargill, M. H. *Modern Canadian English Usage: Linguistic Change and Re-construction.* Toronto: McClelland and Stewart, 1974.

Tormey, Kieran P. "Abbreviations in Formal English Writing" (Part One). *Termiglobe*, II, 3 (Sept. 1979): 23–24.

————. "Abbreviations in Formal English Writing" (Part Two). *Termiglobe*, II, 4 (Nov. 1979): 31–34.

Vallins, G. H. *Spelling.* Revised by D. G. Scragg. London: André Deutsch, 1954, rev. ed. 1965.

VI   Works relating specifically to reference matter

American Chemical Society. *Bibliographic Guide for Editors and Authors.* Washington, D.C., 1974.

Borko, Harold, and Charles L. Bernier. *Indexing Concepts and Methods.* New York: Academic Press, 1978.

British Union—Catalogue of Periodicals Incorporating World List of Scientific Periodicals / New Periodical Titles 1980. Toronto: Butterworths, 1981.

Collison, Robert L. *Indexes and Indexing.* New York: De Graff, 1972.

Knight, G. Norman. *Indexing, The Art of.* London: Allen Unwin, 1979.

U.S.A. Standards Institute. U.S.A. Standard Z39.4-1968. *Basic Criteria for Indexes.* New York, 1969.

VII Works relating to the elimination of sexual, racial and ethnic stereotyping

Canada. Department of Employment and Immigration. *Canadian Classification and Dictionary of Occupations. Manual of Sex-Free Occupational Titles*. Ottawa, 1977.

—————— . Department of Employment and Immigration. *Status of Women. Editorial Guidelines*. Ottawa, 1983.

—————— . Department of National Health and Welfare. *Guidelines for the Elimination of Sexual Stereotyping in Language and Visual Material*. January 1983.

—————— . Multiculturalism. Department of the Secretary of State. *A Matter of Balance*. Ottawa, 1983.

—————— . Multiculturalism. Department of the Secretary of State. *Visible Minorities and the Media. Conference Report*. Ottawa, 1983.

—————— . Treasury Board. *Administrative Policy Manual*, Chapter 484, "Elimination of sexual stereotyping." Ottawa, 1982.

—————— . Treasury Board. Circular No. 1984-4, "Guidelines for the Representative Depiction of Visible and Ethnic Minorities and Aboriginal Peoples in Government Communications." Ottawa, 1984.

Canadian Advisory Council on the Status of Women. *Guidelines for Non-Sexist Writing*. Ottawa, 1984.

Lakoff, Robin. *Language and Woman's Place*. New York: Harper & Row; 1975; rpt. 1976.

Miller, Casey, and Kate Swift. *The Handbook of Nonsexist Writing*. New York: Harper & Row, 1980.

Sorrels, Bobbye D. *The Nonsexist Communicator*. Englewood Cliffs, N.J.: Prentice-Hall, Inc., 1983.

Index

Abbreviations, 1.01 – 23. *See also* Acronyms
and initialisms
  capitalization of, 1.04
  corporate names, 1.15
  degrees, honours, awards, etc., 1.07
  in footnotes, reference notes and indexes,
    9.13, 9.28, 9.48
  geographical names, 1.08
  hyphenation of, 1.04
  imperial units, 1.23, 5.10
  Latin terms, 1.13
  latitude and longitude, 1.10
  military, 1.06
  monetary units, 1.20, 5.11, 5.26
  months and days, 1.21
  parts of a book or document, 1.12
  periodical titles, 9.16, 9.20
  periods with, 1.02
  plurals of, 1.03
  points of the compass, 1.09
  postal, 1.08
  provinces and territories, 1.08
  scientific and technical terms, 1.14
  streets and buildings, 1.11
  titles of courtesy, 1.05
  titles of office, 1.05
  use of in text, 1.01

Abstract, of a report, 11.07

Acronyms and initialisms, 1.16
  capitalization of, 1.16
  indexing of, 9.39
  plurals of, 1.03
  use of definite article with, 1.16
  use of periods with, 1.02, 1.16

Acts and treaties
  capitalization of names of, 4.07
  footnote citation of, 9.14
  italicization of names of, 6.06
  references to subdivisions of, 5.22, 6.10

Addresses
  abbreviations for, 1.11
  figures used for, 5.21
  in letters, 10.12 – 13
  use of comma in, 7.21

Adjectival expressions
  hyphenation of, 2.04
  use of figures in, 5.05

Age, numbers used for, 5.15

Agenda, 11.20 – 21

Aircraft, names of. *See* Ships, aircraft, automo-
biles, etc., names of

Ampersand, 1.18 *See also* Corporate names

Annunciatory expressions
  use of colon with, 7.29
  use of comma with, 7.15(e)

Any, every, no and *some*, compounds formed with,
2.08

Apostrophe, 7.60 – 67
  to form plurals, 1.03, 7.67
  to form possessives, 7.60
  with contractions, 7.65 – 66

Appositives, use of comma with, 7.15(d)

Astronomical terms, 4.22

Awards. *See* Degrees, honours, awards, etc.

Bible, references to books of, 4.18, 5.22

Bibliographies, 9.17 – 28
  alphabetization of entries in, 9.21
  arrangement of, 9.18
  article entry in, 9.20
  examples of types of entries, 9.22, 9.23,
    9.25 – 27
  monograph entry in, 9.19
  in reports, 11.10
  translated and transliterated titles in, 9.24
  types of, 9.17

Billion, use of, 5.26

Books
  bibliographical entries for, 9.19
  footnote references to, 9.06
  references to parts of, 1.12, 4.33, 5.22
  titles capitalized, 4.28, 9.06, 9.19
  titles italicized, 6.05, 9.06, 9.19

  Braces, 7.42 – 43

  Brackets, 7.40 – 41

**Canadian Permanent Committee on
Geographical Names**, I.i

Capitalization, 4.01 – 34
  of abbreviations and acronyms, 1.04, 1.16, 4.27
  of academic degrees, 4.11
  of astronomical terms, 4.22
  of biological classifications, 4.23
  of compass points, 4.20
  of cultural periods, movements and styles, 4.15
  of definite article, 4.29
  of family appellations, 4.09
  general uses, 4.01
  of geographical terms, 4.20
  of governments and government bodies, 4.05
  of headings, 11.12
  of historical periods and geological eras, 4.14
  of hyphenated compounds, 4.31
  of index entries, 9.41